# P.S. I Forgive You

## A Broken Legacy

## D.G.Kaye

# Copyright © D.G. Kaye 2016

Trade Paperback Release: September 2016
ISBN: 978-0-9947938-2-9 Paperback

# Disclaimer

*P.S. I Forgive You* is a work of nonfiction. The author has used her best recollections of events that took place in her life in the writing of this book, conveyed to the best of her knowledge. In order to maintain anonymity, some names have been changed.

# Dedication

I dedicate this book to my brothers and sister.

We endured. We survived. We're okay.

# Acknowledgments

My thanks to author Sally Georgina Cronin for taking time out of her busy life to read this book in its early stages, offering her valuable input, and leaving me with her empowering words of wisdom, which reminded me to be proud of who I am and how far I've come.

I'd also like to thank my best friend Zan for her advice as a reader and for her insightful feedback. Thanks also to my sister-in-law Katie for her insights and feedback during the process of designing the cover of this book.

Thanks as always to my publishing team:

Talia Leduc – Editor
Yvonne Less – Cover Design: art4artists.com.au
Jo Robinson – eBook and Paperback Design: Indie Author Support Services

# Also Written by D.G. Kaye

*Conflicted Hearts*
*A Daughter's Quest for Solace from Emotional Guilt*

*Words We Carry*
*Essays of Obsession and Self-Esteem*

*MenoWhat? A Memoir*
*Memorable Moments of Menopause*

*Have Bags, Will Travel*
*Trips and Tales – Memoirs of an Over-packer*

# Editorial Review

"It is challenging to write about emotional pain and to revisit events, a time when you felt powerless. Not everyone is courageous enough to undertake such a task. D.G. Kaye bravely faces her childhood and relationship with her mother, sharing this complex experience with us in her memoir *P.S. I Forgive You: A Broken Legacy*.

Kaye writes from a place of maturity and strength, bringing hope to others who need to find forgiveness to heal." — **Sally Cronin, *Turning Back the Clock***

# Contents

*Narcissism is a disease that inhibits the ego*

*and bleeds the souls of its victims.*

# Introduction

*P.S. I Forgive You* is a journey in understanding the psychological power my narcissistic mother held over me. Writing it has been my quest to relinquish residual hurts and find forgiveness for both her and myself as her death approached—despite the wrongs she committed.

Although this book was originally intended as a sequel to *Conflicted Hearts*, it stands alone in its own right as a new journey of discovering and overcoming my mother's narcissism, delving into what propelled her, and, ultimately, learning to forgive her for her emotional abuse and to forgive myself for carrying blame and deeply rooted guilt, for believing I wasn't good enough as a daughter because I didn't stay till her bitter end.

This story is the completion of a lifecycle, the cutting of a cord with all its frayed ends.

Many decades passed before I realized the invisible hold my mother had on me. Narcissistic parents have a special way of stunting their children's self-esteem because they'll go to any lengths to keep themselves in the spotlight and demean anyone who questions their actions.

As a young child, I endured the wrath of my mother's reign. I had no choice. I'd dance to her tune or pay the price with hurtful words and threats. If I were to comment on anything she said or roll my eyes in distaste, I was an ungrateful little girl and would be sent to my room in punishment for disobeying her. My mother rarely missed the opportunity to sting me with a dose of guilt in any confrontation.

I did my best to stay out of her orbit, hoping she wouldn't assign me some new chore or call upon me as a messenger to deliver nasty threats to my father. Playing outside, no matter the season, was my solace. As I grew into my teens, though, I began to spend most of my time in my room. I liked it there. By then, my small black and white TV, the telephone on my nightstand, and my sacred 45s and record player became my company when I'd hide out in my place of refuge. Going to my room was no longer a punishment. It had become my safe haven.

At eighteen, I managed to move away from home in search of peace and a chance to make a life for myself. I thought by living on my own, I was escaping my mother, but that wasn't the case. A narcissistic mother doesn't have to be in one's presence. She can still demand and demean no matter how far away.

After several attempts to break free from her only to then allow her back repeatedly in hopes she might have learned something from the separation, nothing changed. My mother had a crafty way of laying on the guilt to snare me back into her lair.

My mother didn't mother with love. She used threats, guilt, and blackmail to hold me under her power. The love I once held for her as a child, when I didn't know any better, eventually grew into pity. It became difficult for me to give love when I'd never received it.

I have overcome many emotional hurdles to get where I am today, and I spent several years thinking I was a bad daughter because of my conditioning. I did everything Mother asked of me so as not to disappoint, and if I was ever unable, she conveniently reminded me that I never did anything for her. Such was our lifecycle until she finally broke me, and even after I left her for the last time, I felt like a bad daughter because of it. However, with encouragement from good friends and my siblings, I grew to learn I was not responsible for my mother's unhappiness. I was responsible for my own.

I was determined not to allow my mother to transfer her wickedness to me. Just because she was my mother, I didn't have to follow in her footsteps. Hurting people's feelings and stepping on those who dared to outshine her weren't admirable habits. I have learned by her example and from the emotional wounds she inflicted on me how important it is to be kind and compassionate. I understand how it feels to be held captive and manipulated by a narcissist.

I am free now. I have forgiven myself for banishing my mother years before her death. My years of tormenting myself with guilt after finally turning my back on my mother have turned into resolve with understanding and the knowledge that my mother's behavior wasn't my fault. Her shortcomings as a mother did not define who I am. Her demons were her own to live with.

After reflecting on what I have endured and subsequently accomplished in life, growing healthy relationships and achieving my aspirations, I can now look back with no regrets.

*Those with flawed egos know not what they have wrought.*

# Aftermath

My mother is dead.

She had been dying for so many years that when the day finally came, my heart was drowning in a swirling abyss of guilt. The years of emotional turmoil I had pent up as the daughter of a narcissistic mother had reached their denouement.

My anger and past resentment toward my mother had turned into an inquisition, a searching of my soul. I needed to understand the root of her ego. It was not enough for me to lay her body to rest. I needed to fill in the gaps, find out what had spurred the injustices she inflicted on so many, and clear the debris lingering in my own conscience to make peace with my past and send her off with my forgiveness.

I had realized how emotionally toxic it was to hang on to hurt and resentment, but the death of my emotionally abusive mother didn't necessarily end the residual hurt of being abused. To set my heart free, I needed to seek out a path to resolve past hurts and the conflict that had tainted my memories.

I'll never know if peace waits for my mother on the other side. I wonder if the afterlife offers second chances to wrongdoers or if they learn lessons from the injustices they commit while on earth. I'd like to think God has mercy and has welcomed my mother into heaven with the same forgiveness I have granted her after learning to surrender my resentments. Looking back, I have realized what a lost soul my mother really was.

Through all her theatrics, lies, and betrayals as she portrayed herself as the person she wanted to be, or perhaps believed she was, my mother harbored a damaged soul that didn't know how to dig itself out. The same persona she had created to shine in the limelight, to acquire anything she desired, or to disguise her insecurities ironically became her downfall.

This story is the aftermath, my way of coming to terms with and relinquishing the guilt and instilled fears I have carried from childhood. It is my decision to banish my mother from my life and a resolution to find peace within myself with my decision.

# Ego

Throughout my mother's lack of attention toward me in my childhood and despite my decision to walk away from her, she remained a huge presence in my conscience.

What did I know about narcissism? As a child, I had neither heard the term nor realized it was the clinical description for my mother's behavior. However, as I grew older and began studying my mother, I learned that her obsession with her image and her lack of consideration for the feelings of others did have a name. My mother was indeed a narcissist, complete with all the classic symptoms.

Dictionaries have varying definitions for this disorder. I could tick off in agreement many of the traits that applied to my mother. To name a few: self-centeredness, an inflated sense of entitlement, admiration of her own mental and physical attributes, a willingness to stoop to any lengths to obtain what she wanted with no regard for others and to steamroll anyone in her way with lies and belittling if she perceived that person as a threat to her superiority, a lack of empathy, ruthlessness, and a tendency to dominate relationships.

What I found most disturbing, though, was that behind her facade lay a fragility my mother tried desperately not to acknowledge to herself, as it was a painful reminder that the status she had built up in her own imagination was only a cover for who she really was.

My mother portrayed herself as delightful and socially charming, yet she presented her true manipulative, overbearing self when there was nobody around to impress. As the child of a narcissist, I was often emotionally neglected because my mother had neither the time nor the capacity to love anyone but herself. She grew to resent my siblings and me as we grew older and wiser. It seemed the more we came to learn about her, the more threatened she felt and the more she worried she would no longer be able to lord her mightiness over us. She didn't like the fact that we were on to her and her games.

Her jealousy of her children escalated as the years passed. In particular, I noted that my mother became jealous of me, her own daughter, as I grew out of my awkward teenage looks and began maturing into a young woman. She despised the fact that time was catching up with her appearance while her daughter was blooming with a beauty that threatened to surpass her own.

My mother became envious of the relationships her children had with their spouses and the time we spent with our extended families. As my siblings and I learned when we wished to share some of our lives with her, she wasn't interested in hearing about things that didn't involve her. Her snide comments about how we cared more about our spouses and their families than about her were enough to stop us from wanting to share anything else.

My mother thrived on attention, male attention in particular. My male friends were no exception. I wrote in my first book about how it felt for me to bring home a male friend to do homework together after school. In junior high, still going through my awkward stage, with no self-esteem, I was secretly crushing on that boy. Rare as it was for my mother to be home during the day, it was my luck that she was home then, and my hopes of gaining his attention were dashed once he met her. He was smitten with her beauty and flirty words. It was part of her DNA to flirt with men and gain their adoration. I felt invisible in her presence.

My mother continued to crave the limelight with the men I dated over the years, and I witnessed her in action plenty of times. When I introduced her for the first time to the man who is now my husband, she didn't abstain from her usual behavior. He was handsome and jovial, and he happened to be two years older than she was. When our relationship became serious, I thought it proper to introduce him to her, and he kindly invited her to dinner with us.

Within moments of meeting him, she leaned over to me in the restaurant and whispered, "Where did you find him? He's my type of man, and he's more my age." I stared at her as if to say, *I can't believe you even thought that, let alone said it,* and proceeded to look at the menu. It was the usual way I handled my mother: no commenting back, just an eye roll or a glare. I had to ignore her comments and move on.

No words of encouragement ever passed her lips, no congratulations and certainly never a word in apology. That was my mother, a classic case of narcissism, though she didn't know it and most probably wouldn't have even understood what the word meant. Even if she were familiar with the term, she would most definitely have denied that it applied to her even though her personality fit all the criteria. Like all narcissists who refuse to admit defeat once the gig is up, when people slowly began to exit her life and her empire crumbled, my mother began to hate the reality of what was left of her life. In retaliation for her unhappiness, she spread her hatred to whoever remained.

In my mother's case, she had only her four children left to rule with her mighty thrashing words—and then she no longer had even them.

# God Rest Your Soul

When it becomes unhealthy, it's time to leave.

I prayed for my mother every day. After our last breakup, I prayed for her to heal physically and mentally and be free from suffering. I prayed for her to let go of her hatred and resentment toward everyone, and I prayed for her soul to find peace in her next life.

The hardest part was remaining faithful to my decision not to go back to her in her final hours. I had made peace with her within myself, and I didn't want to tarnish that with another round of viciousness, which would have left me to start my healing process over again.

# Karma

The petite, dark-haired woman in the long black dress welcomed me into a small, sunny room, sparse of furniture. She invited me to sit on one of the pillows on the floor. I sat cross-legged inhaling a mist of jasmine smoke from the burning incense on the short, black table in front of me. I listened.

According to the psychic and seer of past lives whom I was recommended to visit while in Sedona, Arizona, in early September of 2014, it was up to me to break the bad karma.

After revealing events that were to occur in my life in the coming year, Rayne granted me three questions. Being the skeptic I am, I was careful not to reveal much when having the reading done, merely nodding in affirmation when she said something accurate pertaining to my life. Then I proceeded to ask her my questions, the third of which was the most important.

Not wanting to divulge anything, I simply asked Rayne, "What about my mother?"

"What about her?" Rayne replied. She stared deep into my eyes with an inquisitive raised eyebrow. Her questioning face indicated she was waiting for more, but she continued to tell me she didn't feel my mother's presence in my life.

I held her gaze for a moment, but I didn't offer another word.

Rayne took a large ancient deck of cards out of a black velvet bag. Shuffling the cards, she informed me these were not regular tarot cards but her personal set, handed down to her from past generations from her home in Thailand.

Dominating thoughts of my mother plagued me with guilt once again while I focused on Rayne dividing the cards into piles. I kept dwelling on the last time I had abandoned my mother. Now, during a reading seven years later, I knew she would not live out the year, and my thoughts tortured me with indecision. Was I obligated to see her and say goodbye before she died? Though I knew it would be a fruitless exercise, as she would only subject me to more verbal abuse, I couldn't manage to shake the guilt I carried.

Rayne continued to place her cards in a random magical order, then raised her eyes to meet mine. In a soothing voice, she confirmed the truth: "Your mother is not in your life." Then she added,

"No, you don't have to go back, but you must pray for her."

A feeling of relief ran through me. It was as though she'd read my mind, confirming my worries but consoling me with her affirmation. It was okay not to go back. After Rayne made that statement, I opened up and shared some thoughts with her. She had pegged the question that had plagued me every day during those few months before my mother would die. I shared that I'd already been praying for my mother every day for seven years even though we weren't speaking. Rayne again confirmed that this was all I needed to do.

Then, while staring at the cards in contemplation, Rayne informed me that my mother and I had been mortal enemies in a past life. Vague as that statement was, I could almost understand it. She said, "Your mother hasn't learned her life lessons in this or her past life, and your conflicts together haven't been resolved in your present lives." She paused for a moment, then added, "You didn't choose to be born to your family. You were sent there." Rayne didn't elaborate on that. The past life she had touched on was not part of my reading package, but she told me she was sharing those facts because they were so prominent in the cards.

My curiosity had me wanting more, but neither time nor money permitted it, as a past-life regression would have involved an hour and a half and several hundred dollars more. I didn't want to abuse her power or seem like I was trying to weasel out any extra information, but I was compelled to ask Rayne why I had been sent to my family. She replied, "You were sent there to teach your mother life lessons."

Rayne reminded me again to keep praying for my mother. She explained that praying for her soul while she was alive would break the bad karma between us that had carried over into this life. She said, "You will be set free by praying for your mother, and she will learn her lessons after she leaves this world."

I took solace in Rayne's words. My intuition has always led me to believe I have a sense of an inner knowing, and that knowing strangely reminds me of the invisible hold my mother has always had on me. Somehow, this tiny piece of understanding from Rayne made me realize just how big life is, and it left me wondering whether my prayers would eventually help my mother find peace in the next realm.

My body felt a calm and peace from my former agitated state of conflict. Rayne's confirmation managed to ease a weight from my soul. It was okay for me not to go back.

Six weeks later, my mother died.

# Mother

After publishing *Conflicted Hearts* while my mother was still living, I was uncertain about my decision to remain distant from my mother before she died. I thought writing that book might help to release the guilt I carried, but the burden of it was not something I could release easily. Much had been left unsaid, and I was unable to gauge my truest feelings until her death.

I chose to omit information about my mother both from our lives and from *Conflicted Hearts*. My underlying fear was that she might read the book, and at the time I wasn't willing to deal with the probable repercussions. My emotions were a mixed bag weighing heavy on my subconscious as I struggled to maintain my decision to keep myself estranged from my mother as her end drew nearer.

I delved deep inside my conscience in an effort to assess my honest feelings after removing the invisible blinders I had chosen to wear to avoid thinking about her. I wanted to seek answers to questions about my childhood, about her childhood. My burning desire to learn what had driven my mother to the life she had led, sheltered inside her own ego, had plagued me for years. As I studied the influences of her rule on me, I struggled to understand why my life with her had been so complicated. Through that journey, I learned forgiveness.

There were questions I never dared ask her, either for fear she'd explode in a tantrum just for my asking or because I knew her answers would be inflated by her desire to paint herself in the best light.

My mother had only one sibling remaining of six, my Aunty Lee. Although I wasn't comfortable pressuring my aunt to divulge secrets about her sister, as my aunt honored the code of sisterhood, she was the last living person who could shed light on my mother's past, so I thought it was time to open the door to some of those conversations. Aside from receiving updates on the ongoing status of my mother's deteriorating health from Aunty Lee, I wanted to hear her thoughts about what had spurred my mother to become the narcissistic person she was.

My brother Rory read *Conflicted Hearts* in the first hours following its publication. Although it was a difficult read for him, taking him back to some painful memories of our childhoods, he let me know how proud he was of me for writing it, but he also didn't hesitate to tell me that I hadn't given enough descriptive examples about the terrible things our mother had done to us. "You should have told more," he said.

At first, I told Rory I couldn't bring myself to write detailed accounts of our mother's behavior while she was still living. As time passed, though, after I had mulled over all my hurt and shed many tears, I realized telling those awful stories wasn't about retaliating and exploiting my mother's faults. I needed to share my story because dealing with a parent with a psychological illness is relevant to many people who may be curious to learn what propels a mother to act as mine did. As my own curiosity deepened, I was compelled to learn what had caused my mother to become who she had become.

In reviewing my life with that woman, I empathized with her lonely existence. My pathos grew immensely as I realized how sad, lost, and alone my mother was despite her grand facade of greatness. My mother's neediness for love and attention transformed her into a dominant force, commanding attention with the only means she had: her physical beauty. That charm worked on others, but my siblings and I were aware of who she was without an audience.

Her pleasure in life, which helped her avoid accepting herself for who she was, was gambling: cards, horseracing, bingo, slot machines... Her desire to win was an ongoing chase, an adrenaline rush. As she grew older, those sports became her last friends, her company, her diversion from an empty life—her last means of excitement.

When I finally ended contact with her, I foolishly believed I'd have a reprieve from her constant badgering, but the guilt I carried from banishing my mother never seemed to subside even without contact. I knew I would most likely have to pay the piper in some form when she died, but I wasn't sure just how her death would play with my emotions.

# Mending Fences

I had lunch with my youngest brother, Robby, a few weeks before publishing my first book in December of 2013. I hadn't seen him in almost a year, and although I called him every so often to check on the status of our mother's health, our conversations were strained with several moments of dead air. Our once close relationship had dwindled through the years after he became our mother's sole caretaker following my estrangement from her. I surmised that this punishment had hampered his meek spirit and caused him to form a growing resentment toward me.

I asked Robby if we could meet for lunch because I wanted to let him know about my upcoming book and make sure he was comfortable with me publishing it. The lunchtime rush passed, and the restaurant was relatively quiet as I sat in discomfort across the table from him, making small talk. The discomfort reminded me of how I had always felt in the presence of my mother, like a stranger searching for something to say, only now I was feeling it with Robby.

Those first few moments in his presence felt awkward. My insides stirred. I wished I could turn back the clock to a different time when Robby and I had been close allies. The past few years had created an invisible wall between us. Fidgeting in my purse as though looking for something, I mentally rehearsed how I was going to open the conversation about how our mother was doing. The question had become a delicate subject between us because I felt damned either way, caught in the middle of two lousy outcomes. I sincerely wanted to keep abreast of the state of her health, but I was concerned Robby would see me as a traitor for asking about her without wanting to be a part of her life. On the other hand, if I didn't ask, he might judge me as callous and uncaring.

I drew a deep breath and summoned the courage to ask him. After receiving the news about her current condition, I asked whether her evil temper had mellowed with the knowledge that she wasn't long for this earth or if she remained relentless in her resolve to demean and act bitter toward those in her orbit. He told me she was as nasty as always. Once again, I was reminded of the awful predicament I'd left Robby in when I had chosen to cut contact. I knew his inner turmoil had been piqued with the onus of taking care of our mother. Her toxic verbal wrath had taken its toll on all four of us, but Robby no longer had anyone with whom to share his load.

I could tell by the moments of silence between us that his resentment had grown in the past few years. Robby didn't have to say it. He isn't a man of many words, and he tends to compartmentalize things the same way I do. Only my inner knowledge of his temperament allowed me to understand his anguish. His once easygoing nature had turned into a strained tolerance as he reached his limit from putting up with my mother's antics and demands.

Robby had once been a boy who never used the word *no* and was full of compassion, but the years he had spent saddled with our mother and her verbal pummeling had soured him. He mentioned having learned how to hang up on her, a task neither he nor I had ever previously mastered. He said his conscience no longer guilted him at it because he knew she'd always call him back the next day. After all, she had nobody else left.

I had no appropriate words of consolation for him. The guilt I carried at leaving him on his own with her had never dissipated. I was sad for our childhoods and the residual emotional carnage all of us had experienced, and I was sad for my mother, who had chased her children away.

Robby made it clear he had no interest in reading my book. He congratulated me and let me know he didn't mind that I had written it and was going to publish it, but he didn't wish to revisit the past. I completely understood his feelings, and I respected them. After a few hours passed, Robby and I aired some of our grievances with one another, and I felt optimistic about the possibility that we had made good strides toward reconciling our broken bond.

# Tell Me Your Secrets

Aunty Lee called me to congratulate me on the publication of my first book a few months after its release. It had been quite a while since I last saw her, and we planned to meet for lunch together. I was relieved and elated to learn she was eagerly waiting for a copy of my book, as I had been concerned her distance over the past few months signified her disapproval at my having written about her sister.

I was delighted to spend a few hours with my last remaining aunt and catch up on our lives. Naturally, we discussed my mother. I questioned her, asking why she thought my mother had never changed from her pretentious self all the way to the bitter near end of her life. My aunt told me my mother was still telling lies and spreading nasty tales about people to whoever would listen, including her. My mother still cursed her children with terrible names in her venomous rants, yet, within the same breath, she would manage to ask

Aunty Lee if she knew why we, her children, no longer spoke to her. I didn't know if she was still playing games or if her stubborn ego wouldn't allow her to acknowledge our reasons.

I appreciated my aunt's candor. She reminded me of a time almost ten years earlier when she had reprimanded my siblings and me for not speaking to our mother even though she knew well our reasons. She had told us repeatedly that respecting our mother was just the right thing to do. I had to wonder, what constituted the right thing now?

Aunty Lee admitted she'd finally stopped asking us to make amends with our mother because she realized what we'd all lived through and were still living through, and she admitted that she didn't want to push her four nieces and nephews out of her own life by judging our decisions, as it wasn't her place to do so. I was grateful that as much as she wished for amends, she had accepted that she didn't have the power to fix something that had been broken for so many years, especially when she had firsthand experience from having endured an entire life with my mother.

A few hours had passed since we finished eating our lunch, but we remained, drinking several cups of coffee in the empty restaurant, as the lunch crowd had long dissipated. We talked about many things, particularly our family history. I often wish I could have had that conversation with her years before, but my grievances with her sister had been a sore subject with her then. The past few years seemed to have awakened her to the reality that my mother wasn't a nice person.

Aunty Lee filled my ears with stories from my mother's past, and, quite honestly, many of them didn't surprise me. In fact, some I'd already heard, while many others I had sensed. My aunt was surprised at how much I knew about my mother's shenanigans from when I was a younger girl—but I had studied her for decades by that point.

Aunty Lee confirmed my suspicions about some of the affairs my mother had had with various men, and there had been quite a few. I had been fully aware of my mother's patterns whenever there was a new lust interest in her life. My aunt divulged that my mother had had numerous affairs not only during my parents' separations but also while they supposedly had been together. The news didn't shock me.

Aunty Lee's stories had me recalling the many nights my mother would saunter into the house late in the evening, well after the racetrack closed at five. In my younger years, I didn't account for the missing hours because I was used to her absences, not yet suspecting her adulterous ways. Later, as I approached my teen years, I figured things out.

I knew who the players were, most of them racetrack acquaintances. I was unsuspecting as a child when my mother would sometimes take us to the track on a Sunday and proudly introduce us to her rich horse-owner friends. As it turned out, some of them happened to be more than just friends. I recalled one of her love interests in particular, whose wife she had conveniently befriended so she could have an excuse to invite their family over on a Sunday. My mother was quite crafty at orchestrating plans. My siblings and I would play with the kids while the adults indulged in cocktails and chitchat. There was no end to how far my mother would go in plotting her deceit.

My mother was a wonderful actress in her own right. My siblings and I would often laugh with one another after witnessing her Academy Award–winning performances while she had an audience, completely different to how she was at home. We'd have a good chuckle at what we called her pretendy voice, a tone an octave higher than her usual, with a hint of jubilance, which she used when trying to charm someone. She thought she was a star and reveled in the attentions men paid her. We were mere characters in her theater.

We were all obedient children, and on the rare occasions we happened to be out with our mother, people often complimented her on how well behaved we were. They had no clue the mother they were flattering wasn't the same person we lived with at home. They didn't know that we didn't dare step out of line because we knew what punishments we'd receive at home if we did.

I discussed with my aunt my observations of the several men I suspected my mother had dated, and she denied not one of them. Our conversation reminded me once again about how much grief my father had endured from my mother, yet that had never stopped him from loving her, despite the broken pieces of his heart that would never mend.

My mother's bitterness at the world escalated with the passing years. She couldn't accept that her performances no longer attracted a captive audience as she aged. The lack of money flowing in had clipped her wings. My father was dead, the men who had swooned over her and given her jewels and money eventually discovered her manipulating ways and left, and my brothers stopped contributing to her gambling addiction. She could no longer conceal her rage with the facade she had projected in past decades. Her jealousies and resentments had surmounted, leaving her as one giant ball of hatred, living in her own self-imposed hell.

***

It's strange how life and death play out. Two months after my mother's passing, my seemingly healthy Aunty Lee was shockingly diagnosed with terminal stomach cancer. Consequently, I spent a lot of time with her in her palliative days along with my sister, Melanie. We laughed together, cried together, and talked about the old days. Aunty Lee was a beautiful soul who looked upon her death head on, fearlessly.

She never had a bad word to say about anyone, including her sister, and she was one of the very few people left in the world who would visit my mother and call her often even when she knew all she would hear were poisonous rants and trash talk. My mother had hurt my aunt many times throughout their lives, yet my aunt refused to abandon her. I hadn't realized how much Aunty Lee tolerated because I had been so caught up in my own web with my mother.

Aunty Lee had gotten the short stick in life, her presence always overshadowed by my mother's. She had watched my mother manipulate people to attain everything she wanted and had listened to her stories, her boasts about her adventures, and she had always managed to compliment my mother when she flaunted her newest baubles in her face. Despite my mother's gloating, my aunt never had a jealous word to say. She was happy for her sister. Aunty Lee never hurt anyone and remained stoic when it came to defending her family against unkind words. I couldn't fathom how two sisters could be so different from one another in their compassions and values.

I continued to visit my aunt in her last weeks. Even though her eyelids weighed heavy and she was weary from an increasing dose of morphine, we still gabbed and laughed at funny memories. There was so much I wanted to ask her about the past she kept buried in her memory, yet I didn't want to cross any lines or invade her privacy. Every now and then, she volunteered some information by telling a story. For instance, I was shocked to learn about the time my mother had left me alone at two months old to run off with some random man to Las Vegas. The story was vague, and when I asked who looked after me in my mother's absence, Aunty Lee couldn't remember, only adding that my heartbroken dad had gone to search for her and had finally brought her home.

As Aunty Lee grew wearier, it seemed many more stories would be left with no endings. I asked her what she thought had made my mother become the person she had, and I wondered whether she might have been beaten or abused. I was grateful when my aunt denied the possibility. Apparently, none of the six siblings had been physically abused, but through my aunt's stories, without her admitting as much, I detected that they had suffered emotional neglect from their parents.

It also became apparent to me, through learning about their childhood, that my mother, the youngest of the six, had learned from her own mother how to manipulate people by using her looks. My mother lost her mother when she was fourteen, but she had experienced a lack of guidance and poor financial status even before then, and these were likely significant factors in her desire to become more than where she had come from. Certainly, a child with no parental direction had passed on to her own children the only thing she knew: emotional neglect.

Aunty Lee stated she too had often wondered how my mother could have grown into such a narcissistic and manipulative person. She told me nobody else was like that in her family, but that left me wondering if their mother was indeed the narcissist my mother had chosen to emulate. Many stories my aunt shared had given me that impression of my grandmother, although I felt Aunty Lee had not realized as much.

I had spent my life trying to analyze my mother and her antics and had come to my own conclusions. There's an old saying: The apple doesn't fall far from the tree. In many circumstances, this holds true. People are often products of their environments and take on familiar traits in their own personalities. Some traits are not admirable, but if we're lucky enough to realize the bad, we have the opportunity to steer ourselves in a better direction. I am lucky to have realized the deficiencies in my upbringing. I made a choice to go against the grain, learning instinctively as I began to mature that what I had experienced of my mother's character was not necessarily good.

I had once been no different than everyone else who knew my mother, captivated by her outer beauty. As a child, I wished to one day be and look like her, desiring for people to adore me the same way they did her. It was entrancing to be out with her, to watch people flock to her, vying for her attention. What shallow thinking that was. It wasn't until I was a teen that I grew to understand, from studying her carefully, how she used her looks to win favor and seek attention. I saw how many people she hurt with lies and insults to obtain what she wanted. I watched my father's heart break countless times when she pretended to be affectionate with him just to obtain something.

Dad had turned to me for consoling many times. Those heartbreaking moments remain vivid in my memory. I'll never forget when Dad took the opportunity to spend a few extra moments with me in the car after dropping us kids back home from a visit with him while my parents were separated. He asked me, his seven-year-old little girl, if I would please ask Mommy if she would take him back. My heart ached for his sadness. I loved my daddy and would have done anything to stop his hurt, even knowing I would pay a price for meddling. However, even as a young child, I felt the request was unfair. My father had burdened me with more worry about confronting my mother, knowing there would be more heartache when she refused me. When I asked my mother if she would allow my dad to come home, she screamed at me with fire in her eyes and slapped my face, telling me it wasn't my business. All the while, she never realized that it was. I wanted to know why she kept sending him away, why she was always mad at him, why he couldn't live with us. She never gave me an answer.

I was grateful for the revelation that I never wanted to be like her. It wasn't in my nature to use people and run over their feelings to get what I wanted. I'd seen too much hurt already.

My mother had a need for attention and materialistic things to make her feel special. Her desires stemmed from envy of those who had more than she did. She was compelled to have the most so she could feel superior. Certainly, her warped view of the world had grown into her narcissistic behavior. Instead of working for and earning what she desired, she thought it far easier to obtain things by flaunting her feminine charms, and when she didn't want to wait for Mr. Right to come along, she focused on creating him.

I thought I knew the story of my parents' year of marriage, which all my aunts had confirmed, but then I heard an earful from Aunty Lee. I empathized with my father because of his unrequited love for my mother, but it appeared there was more to that story.

The truth was that my mother had, in fact, been in love with my dad's best friend before they got married. When the man didn't succumb to the flirting and games she used to gain his attention and affections in hopes he'd break up with his girlfriend, who subsequently became his wife, my mother dug deeper into her arsenal of deceit. She was relentless when she wanted something.

She plotted to retaliate for her unreciprocated feelings by vying for my father's attention, plotting to make his friend jealous. My father was used all the way to the altar, and the saga continued. My poor dad was a pawn in a master game orchestrated by my mother.

I don't believe my mother ever understood what true love meant. Obviously, her incapacity to love carried through into her lack of mothering skills. I'm not sure my aunt even realized how unscrupulous my mother had been in their younger days. Aunty Lee had been humble and content just to have such a popular sister, and through all my mother's gloating, often making my aunt feel inferior, Aunty Lee stood by her side and applauded her successes. Truly, Aunty Lee honored the code of sisterhood.

I wished I hadn't waited so many years to approach my aunt with questions about the past, but I gathered what I could without pushing boundaries, hoping not to put her in the uncomfortable position of feeling like a tattletale. I was grateful that Aunty Lee generously opened up and shared with me with what little time she had left, almost as though she realized that after her death, nobody else would be able to tell those stories.

There isn't much left of my once large maternal family. Aunty Lee was the last of six siblings to die, and her death left my siblings, a few cousins, and me as the eldest generation of our family. Sadly, after Aunty Lee's passing, no more secrets about my mother and my own young life would be revealed. I'm certain many more went to the grave with her.

# Memories

Some people have the ability to pack away painful memories, wedging them tightly in the backs of their minds. Others tend to carry them in the forefront, and this tactic causes the proverbial chip on the shoulder. The weight is a constant reminder of inflicted wounds left unresolved, left to fester and ooze into our daily lives and attitudes if not acknowledged and treated. Emotional pain leaves behind an unhealthy haunting for its victims. My siblings and I carried our hurts differently.

I chose to conquer my demons by getting to know them and facing them head on, mentally reliving situations and dissecting the reasoning behind them. I wanted to know why. Why did bad things happen to us? Why did a mother who was supposed to be our nurturer instead hurt us, whether intentionally or unintentionally? People who unintentionally hurt others possess some sort of psychological disability that shields them from admitting a truth about themselves. In my mother's case, her narcissistic personality wouldn't allow her to understand that her hurtful words and actions left residual wounds beyond comprehension.

This was not normal behavior. Because every action has a reaction, I was convinced my mother's aimless upbringing had steered her to compensate for what she had lacked as a child. Her incapability of loving anyone but herself had to have developed from a lack of emotional nurturing.

Not many days pass that I don't review internal snapshots of my life. My father's portrait hangs proudly on my office wall. His picture has moved with me to every home I've lived in since his death. I glance at his gentle smiling face daily. Sometimes I bounce ideas and dilemmas off him while smiling back at him, and sometimes tears spring from the empty part of my heart that reminds me he's no longer here in this world, taken much earlier than he should have been.

For many years, I didn't display any photos of my mother. At first, my anger toward her kept me from wanting to see her face in my living space, but later, after we stopped speaking, I became afraid to look at her. The mere sight of her reminded me of the guilt I harbored for having banished her from my life. The sadness grew within me for what had become of her pitiful, lonely life. Thinking about her was too much for me to swallow, so it was easier not to have photos of her around me.

After my mother's death, my guilty conscience nagged at me, and I decided to put a photo of her up on the mantel. I chose a picture from my wedding. In it, my husband and I along with my three siblings, Rory, Robby, and Melanie, and my mother all posed happily together. *Posing* is an apt word because, from an onlooker's view, we resembled one big happy family. But my siblings and I were feeling our own personal discomforts in our mother's presence.

I can't recall a time I ever felt comfortable around my mother, especially on my wedding day. She never contributed to the planning of my wedding. In fact, throughout my engagement, she was absent from my life. I received only a few phone calls from her. On one of those calls, she asked me to add some of her old gambling friends to my guest list. In my resentment of her neglect to make any effort to share in my joyous occasion, I denied her requests.

It was only in the final weeks before my wedding that my guilt resurfaced. Feeling bad that she'd had no part in the preparations even though she'd never offered a hand, I invited her to come to the final fitting of my wedding gown. Still, the emptiness remained between us, leaving me with that same melancholy feeling I now get every time I look at that picture of her on the mantel, which reminds me there was no bond between us. Although she wore a beautiful smile, I could sense her pain. She was hurting and feeling resentful because of the distance her children kept from her—although she never let on and although we were all together. When I look at that photo, I feel as though she secretly wished she was sitting with her loving children in a loving moment but knew deep inside that it wasn't that way because of her own doing.

The photo resting on the mantel remains, although it's partially hidden by various other pictures of my husband and my darling great-niece. I'm content with it like that. The photo is out in the open, yet my mother's limelight is shadowed, cluttered by the many other pictures in front of it. But it's there.

I think about my mother often, sadly, without any fond memories—just an aching sadness.

*Who was that woman?*
*The woman who wore an invisible veil through life,*
*Masking her true identity from others*
*But mostly from herself.*
*I knew her as Mother.*

My mother's death unveiled many questions and urged me to reach an understanding about her existence. The mystery of my mother had me seeking out answers to riddles I hadn't cared to solve while she lived, mostly because I'd spent so many years trying to avoid her. As her life neared its end, though, my pity for her grew immensely, and my need to understand what made her choose to live such an egotistical and narcissistic life compelled me to investigate her troubled soul.

I couldn't go back. My instincts and the lessons I had learned from past attempts to reconcile cautioned me from falling into the same trap. My knotted insides couldn't withstand another vicious psychological attack from her keen words, but that didn't lessen the empathy I had for her every time I thought about her demise.

During the remaining time my mother had, I worried she might somehow read my book. The fear of it consumed me long before I even published *Conflicted Hearts*. Despite her failing vision and the fact that she had never cared to read, I was concerned she might ask my aunt or brother to bring her a copy if she were to discover its existence. Although there was no vengeance in the book, only truths my mother would never admit to, in denial of who she was, I was afraid she would find a way to punish me if she had a chance to read it. When I shared this fear with my brother Rory, he replied, "What can she do to you? Is she going to hit you or scream at you?" He reminded me that she couldn't do anything to me anymore, and he urged me to stop being afraid of her. Yet I couldn't let go of the fear.

The fear was part of a continuous cycle of guilt she had instilled in me my entire life. I wasn't afraid of being slapped. I was afraid of her hurtful words and the guilt she'd find a way to lay on me. My fears of disobeying her since childhood had never dissipated. Anything she disapproved of came with reprimanding, threats, and demeaning comments. That was my fear. I couldn't have my feelings crushed by her, and I couldn't live with the thought that I'd done something to make her unhappy again. I didn't want to be responsible for her pain.

I was concerned that if she were blatantly confronted with my words, she might discover how others perceived her, which would cause her to go into hysterics and possibly have a heart attack while in the throes of one of her manic protests. I didn't want to be potentially responsible for her death. She had never believed she was anything but perfect, and nobody had ever dared let her know otherwise. My imagination ran wild with scenarios. The possibility of having to carry the added guilt of her death on my shoulders for the rest of my life was unsettling. I had already gone through life second guessing myself, wondering whether the things I did would ignite my mother's wrath at any given time. A book presenting her in her truest form would certainly have been earthshattering to her.

When I continued to share my fears with Rory, he once again retorted, "If she ever read the book, she'd most likely respond with her true theatrical denial and say it's all bullshit, that she isn't that person." He reminded me she had lived in denial about herself her entire life, so why did I think she'd do otherwise now?

As it turned out, Aunty Lee calmed my worries when she told me that my mother could no longer see well enough to read, and she advised that I stop fretting over the situation. However, she also revealed that she had accidentally mentioned, while making small talk with my mother, that I was writing a book. Aunty Lee didn't discuss what the book was about, yet my mother didn't hesitate to comment, "It better not be about me or I'll fucking sue her."

Those are the last loving words of comfort by which I can remember my mother.

# A Letter

*I know your dominating ego won't allow you to like or love, and nor will it allow you to let go of the sorrow you harbor for what your life has become. I know in my soul how depressed and isolated you feel. You won't allow yourself to acknowledge your wrongs. You won't allow us into your heart, yet you broke ours anyway.*

*I weep for you, Mother, for the day you will go to the next world. I'm torn. I pray for you always, for peace and no suffering. All the years of trying to fix you have left me with only prayers as a means to send you love and forgiveness. I know that as your illness progressed, your resentment toward the world for the state in which it left you increased tenfold, but the truth is that you abandoned yourself with the choices you made.*

*You made it unbearably painful for me to come back for one more round of your artillery. Did you ever think your child needed a mother? Did you truly not need me?*

*I sit here writing this while every breath of yours grows shallower. I am not with you. I'm with my family, my brothers and sister. I am praying for your soul, that it may find peace to release you from your self-imposed imprisonment. You've been locked inside yourself for so many years.*

*I wish we could have been friends. I wish you would've allowed yourself to be loved. But, above all, I wish I could have understood what drove you to become the sad, mean-spirited person you are. I wish I could have made you smile.*

*I went to visit Dad today. I needed a parent. I wanted to let him know you'd soon be on your way to fill the empty space in the ground beside him. He has waited for you for so many years. I pray your heart has thawed and you won't disturb his eternity.*

*I wish you a safe journey.*

*With love,*

*Your eldest daughter*

# An Ode

*I have feared you for most of my life,*
*A constant longing to end the strife.*

*I wanted you to own your mistakes.*
*The decades passed, yet your heart wouldn't wake.*

*I shudder and wince when I picture you alone.*
*You left me no choice. The emotional abuse I could*
*no longer condone.*

*I wish you peace, Mama, in the time you have left.*
*I just can't come back. My heart is bereft.*

*Please know that I have wept.*

# Tells and Tales

The engine hummed while we sat in the big white parked Coupe de Ville Cadillac in front of our local variety store. Rory and I waited while our mother ran in to buy a pack of smokes. I was in a foul mood from an earlier reprimanding, and my wounded soul had me blurting out the words "I hate that fucking bitch." No sooner than I had done so, I regretted sharing them aloud for Rory to hear.

"Oh, I'm telling Mom you called her a fucking bitch!" Rory shouted, and he laughed in delight at the thought of what my mother might do to punish me for my heinous crime. I was mortified, petrified at the thought of her finding out. I begged and pleaded with Rory not to tell.

I can't recollect exactly what my brother's silence cost me. Quite possibly I was at his beck and call for favors for a short time while he held his threat over my head. That was the usual exchange between us kids when we blackmailed one another with threats to tell Mom. Ironically, we had mastered blackmail because we had a great teacher.

I couldn't imagine what my mother would do to me if she heard what I'd called her, if she discovered that one of her children didn't worship her. I thought about the time she'd heard me use the word *shit* when I was five years old. She had pulled me into the bathroom and shoved soap in my mouth, and I was horrified at the thought of what she'd do if she heard I had used a more terrible word, this time directed at her.

I was impulsive, still learning to control the angst I harbored because of my mother. I was tired of living my life around her moods and directives. I was barely twelve years old, and at that point I just wanted someone to call her out, to stop allowing her to get away with her bullshit lies and her high and mighty attitude. But nobody talked to her like that. Nobody dared to.

When Rory heard me blurt out those words, I knew he figured he had some good ammunition to use against me, and he used it wisely. At first, I was riddled with fear he'd tell on me, but even while I was bargaining with Rory about my punishment, somewhere in my heart of hearts, I knew he shared my fear of my mother's temper. Deep down inside, he had compassion for me, no matter how tempting the juicy piece of news would have been to share with her.

In that situation, I realized that no matter how much distance had grown between us, Rory still had a spot for me inside his heart. It was enough for me to know that when push came to shove, my brother honored the sacred bond of siblinghood.

As a child, I feared my mother's temper immensely, and it wasn't the type of fear I could grow out of. I dreaded having to ask her anything because the answer and tone would depend on her mood. Relentless screaming and theatrical fits of anger were her usual defenses when confronted with anything that threatened to reveal her nasty demeanor, so I chose not to share my feelings with her. Others did the same.

Aside from the verbal thrashings she dished out, she always managed to plant a seed of guilt in her children. If she wasn't making me feel guilty for something, she was threatening me. Daily life felt like a rollercoaster around my mother. Her moods changed like the winds.

She was seldom home while I was growing up, and when I was a little girl I'd cry to myself, tucked under my covers many nights, because I missed having a mother. By the time I was ten or eleven, I'd learned to live without her and had become grateful for her absence because I took solace in the peace.

While my mother painted the town with her highfalutin lifestyle, I looked after my younger siblings. I cooked, tidied the house, did laundry, and babysat after picking them up from school. If she ever came home from a losing day at the racetrack and I had dared to forget one thing on her list of chores, the fear of God rose within me at what I might expect as punishment. Her shrieking was something I aimed to avoid by obeying her commands.

I wasn't aware that my childhood wasn't normal. It never dawned on me that other kids' moms made their children lunch, or came on school field trips, or even took them to school or picked them up. I never knew that moms made a big fuss about their daughters' first proms or took them out to buy pretty dresses and treated them to nice hairdos at the beauty parlor. Heck, I didn't even know what menstruation was. The first five times I bled when I was eleven, I thought I might have been dying.

I never missed these things because I didn't understand what moms were supposed to do for their daughters. I couldn't miss what I didn't know I didn't have.

# The End Is Near

**M**y mother had been dying for years, and through those years she refused to surrender her bitterness and remained in denial of her flaws. The many times I heard she was dying reminded me of the boy who cried wolf. I almost believed she was invincible, and even though I never wanted her to suffer, she did.

I thought it was just a horrible and sad way to die—holding hatred for those she had chased out of her life, living in bitter seclusion, knowing her days were numbered. Her once vibrant life had diminished into a mere existence of watching TV and complaining. She'd also given all her caregivers a difficult time, bitching at them all and letting them know how useless they were to her because of what her life had become. Nobody was exempt.

I asked my brother Robby why God didn't just take her out of her misery and pain during one of the many times she was on the brink of death. Why would he not spare her from suffering? He replied,

"God has his own plans." I couldn't help but wonder if he was letting her suffer because she had hurt so many people in her lifetime, but in my next thought I couldn't believe God would play those cruel games, tit for tat.

I wondered what thoughts had to have been going through my mother's head. How awful it must have been to know her time left on earth was limited. I thought about how frightened she must have felt in her lonely world, although she'd never admit it. I was sad for her, knowing that the anger and bitterness she displayed was a front for the depressed state of her pathetic life. I couldn't fathom why she remained so obstinate in her resolve to spend what little time she had left wallowing in misery instead of embracing the end and making amends with her children. I wanted to fix her, but I didn't know how.

Her formerly grand life had diminished into a tiny existence. She no longer flaunted her beauty to all who idolized her. Her schemes to extract money from my brothers to support her gambling pleasures were no longer effective. Three of her children had already exited her life because of her verbal abuse. There was nobody left to fall prey to her demands.

I hurt for her. She wasn't much of a mother, but she was still my mother.

I wondered so many things about her. Because she had lived in disguise all her life, I was never certain if she truly believed she was a wonderful person or if she had only spent her life pretending as much. I wanted to ask her, *Do you regret that your children aren't around you? Have you ever admitted to yourself why they are no longer in your life? You've asked us all countless times why we aren't speaking to you. Do you actually not know why, or does your denial not allow you to admit your wrongs? Why haven't you ever apologized? Do you truly believe you've done nothing wrong? Why don't you want to make peace before you die? Why?*

I spoke with my sister, Melanie, the voice of reason, about the mixed emotions I was having regarding our mother's impending death and the guilt I still carried from having abandoned her seven years earlier. Melanie knew the cross I bore for my mother, but she didn't harbor the same guilt I did. She reminded me that us children had all tried to appease our mother all of our lives to no avail, and she added that she couldn't feel sad for our mother because she felt like our mother had already been gone for so many years. In her next breath, though, Melanie admitted that she was sad that she didn't feel sad. It made sense to me.

The updates from my Aunty Lee and Robby about my mother's health always came with fatal warnings, but my mother was a tough bird. She'd already defied death numerous times against countless odds. Still, it was a cruel punishment for a woman who had lived inside her huge ego all her life to become aged and sickly long before old age had set in. I wouldn't have wished my mother's demise on anyone—not even her.

Her vanity had long ago vanished. At seventy-four, after more than a decade of illness, she was fighting just to survive, and that must have eventually taken precedence over her desire to look beautiful. Her once flaming red hair, her crowning glory, was now a gray unkempt mist. Her beautifully chiseled capped porcelain teeth had reached their own expiration date and fallen out, leaving her once rosy high cheekbones sunken. My brother informed me that Mom's legs were blackening with the onset of gangrene, their shape and size comparable to tree trunks. I couldn't erase that vision from my mind every time I thought of her.

My mother was living in a haze of morphine, but she was still in full command of her faculties. She knew what she was saying and continued to defend her lies. She'd been a sociopathic liar long before I was born. According to Robby, her demise only fueled her bitterness and hatred toward everyone in protest for what she had become. Bedridden for the last two years of her life, with the occasional change of scenery moving from the bed to the couch with a walker, she refused to have her legs amputated. Yet she lived.

She fought Robby with every ounce she could muster when he told her it was time to go into a home. She had already lived much longer than the doctors had predicted. In her more adamant years, she had cursed at the possibility of one day having to end up in a home, reminding us all she didn't need anybody to take care of her. Her fiery temperament had previously cautioned us to leave the delicate subject alone, but as her health began to leave her nearly immobilized, we had no option but to move her to where she could get the necessary care and alleviate some of the pressure from Robby.

Her stubborn nature allowed her to remain in her little apartment as long as she could hold out, insisting once again that she was fine on her own, but eventually my mother had to surrender her last hold on her independence and move, at Robby's urging, to a senior home with medical assistance.

My heart filled with sorrow for her the day she moved. I knew her defiance, and no matter what our differences were, I wept for her surrender. But I was also relieved that I wouldn't have to worry about her possibly dying alone one day with nobody at her side, her body left undiscovered for perhaps a day or two. I was, at least, comforted by the thought that she'd be cared for around the clock in that strange place where people leave their homes for a stop along the way before death. I prayed for peace for her every day. I wondered if she knew.

It was so ironic that a woman who had demanded so much from everyone and commanded attention with tantrums and threats was now left a shell of the icon she had once been. She fought to stay alive with such tenacity as each part of her body became more afflicted with illness. I couldn't imagine what her will to live was for. She no longer had a life of any quality. She had no friends, no children or grandchildren coming to visit her, no one but Robby and Aunty Lee. She had a bad heart after two triple bypasses, was breathing only with the aid of an oxygen tank, had gangrenous legs, and was addicted to painkillers. I couldn't fathom what had possessed her with the strength and will to live.

Though the guilt panged away at my heart for not being of any comfort to her in her transition of leaving the home she had known for so many years, the past cautioned me, leaving me unable to look her in the eyes and allow history to repeat itself again. If I could have summoned the courage, I would have asked her why she couldn't be kind. Why had she let the years go by in bitterness? Why could she never be happy for anyone's accomplishments or joys, especially her children's?

Why was everyone and everything looked upon as competition? Why did she feel that others' joy took away from her limelight? Most of all, why did she have to be jealous of her own children instead of being proud of them?

I wanted to ask her, *Mother, if you could no longer be the fairest of them all, why did you have to become so hateful? I know your hatred grew from jealousy. What you couldn't achieve, you couldn't bear to see your children surpass you in. Why was everything always about you? I spent my life trying to know you and understand your shortcomings. I tried to share my life with you with laughter, but you knocked my successes, saying, "You think you're so great." Although you had no interest in my life, I still tried to do right by you as a daughter. I tried to respect you, holding my tongue when you had nothing but darkness to spew. Even through the grief and neglect you gave me, and after my final exit from your life, I still worried about you, about how you believed you were something more than you were. I grieved what was left of you when your party in life was over.*

*I despised what your empty life had become. You couldn't have wanted that, but your pride would never, for just once in your life, have let your false bravado down. Even with nothing, you pretended to yourself that you were still the maestro. You were a figment of your own imagination, yet I wept for you, the you I never knew, the person you didn't want to know.*

*You gave birth to us without a plan or appreciation for the gift of having children or for what it meant to be a mother. Sacrifice wasn't for you because you had spent your life feeling as though the world owed you something grand. You always came first. Everyone else, including your children, was secondary.*

I flinched when I thought of my mother lying there in a world of nothingness, swallowed up by bitterness and pain, yet she was determined to remain alive. I couldn't understand. Why did the thought of dying scare her more than the painful life she was living?

I'd often sit in contemplation about how I'd react to my mother's death when the time came. I knew in my soul that after many warnings over the years, her end was truly approaching now, but I still couldn't imagine myself going back to the chaos that engulfed me with her. Even in her last months, I had been forewarned by Robby and Aunty Lee that despite how much my mother suffered with illness, she refused to let go of her wretched attitude and degradation of others. Her venomous words about her children never ceased, spewed upon any ears allowing her the chance to vent.

I was also concerned about how my siblings would feel and react after my mother's death. Rory and Melanie were well ahead of me in severing ties with our mother, and they were both similar in their reservations. They had their own ways of pushing thoughts of my mother far beyond remorse. I can't say I blamed them, knowing well some of the awful things my mother had done to them.

Robby and I had always been more ridden with guilt. We tended to have empathy for our mother and allowed ourselves to listen to her dirt without comment.

My mother had hurt Rory for the last time eight years earlier, having cut a wound so deep in him that there was no room left for forgiveness. She had let into him for cutting off her gambling allowance and had ripped his heart apart with painful and ugly words in retaliation. My mother had an uncanny way of knowing how to hurt her children when she didn't get her way. Rory said she was already dead to him, but somewhere behind the wall he built to shut her out, I know in my heart that he carried an insurmountable hurt. Rory was a good son to my mother, but she never appreciated his kindness, took his good nature for granted, and finally bit the hand that fed her when he had taken all he could.

As for Melanie, she was a single mom raising three small kids, and when she could have used a little motherly compassion and a helping hand, all she got were complaints and demands for favors. All conversations inevitably led back to my mother's problems, and her addiction to gambling came before any thoughts of babysitting. Her selfishness finally wore thin on Mel.

That was when I inherited my mother, mostly all to myself.

I took her tantrums and demeaning of my siblings and me for a couple of years until I became physically ill from the daily grind. One fateful day, I crested the wave of poison my mother was drowning me with, and I snapped. For almost fifty years, I had let her steamroll me without talking back, but that day I replied. I gave her a lengthy sermon, telling her how much damage and fear she had inflicted on her children with her negligence. I had to let her know just once how much resentment I carried for her self-centeredness and her manipulation of others. I called her out on several of her antics and informed her that her strong arming, blackmail, and lies no longer held power over me. She didn't understand that it was a privilege to be a mother.

Then I hung up on her, and that was the last time I ever heard from or saw my mother.

***

After Rory, Mel, and I banished our mother from our lives a final time, Robby was all she had left. His new position to do battle as my mother's caretaker put an enormous strain on our own relationship. His resentment at having to do everything for her and put up with her antics drove a wedge between us, because I had left him in that position. Her demands grated on Robby as seven years passed with him having been left on his own to take care of her, and this caused an eventual distance in our once close-knit bond. He was the last man standing, and no matter how much he wanted to flee as the three of us had already done, his empathy kept him from abandoning her.

While I was kept abreast of my mother's relentless rants and ploys to demean her children, I was amazed that her heart never softened and that she hadn't at least mellowed in some way. I thought that if she knew her life was nearing an end, she might have some remorse for her behavior, possibly let her guard down, or want to make amends with her children. But she didn't.

Countless times I'd imagine scenarios where I'd be called to her death bed, and I struggled for years wondering if she'd request it or if I'd even go. Her passing was a tragic end of suffering, and she took her bitterness, inflated ego, and beliefs with her to the grave. Her death was the end of an era, leaving behind a formidable legacy.

# Still

Not one day has passed that I haven't thought of my mother. My heart has been burdened with the vision of my mother and her lifeless soul approaching death, replaying in my conscience. The sadness has reminded me that only Robby was by her side, waiting for God to take back her wounded soul to a place of peace from herself and her earthly losses.

I continue to feel her loneliness throughout my own existence while overlooking all the bitterness, because it's the sadness that hurts most. Nobody should have to die in loneliness—not even my mother.

My heart sinks every time I think about having abandoned my mother. I sometimes overlook the validity of my reasons for leaving with every crushing memory. As I sensed her time on earth drawing to an end, I had to remind myself that my intent wasn't to punish her; it was merely to save myself from emotional torture. I had to learn how to think about myself. I know I have to comfortably accept the decisions I've made, but it's difficult when I can't seem to distance myself from what I fled.

I hate pain. Nobody likes pain, and I have a difficult time watching others in pain, as well. I can never seem to find the right words to ease it, and when I can't stop a wounded soul from bleeding, I feel helpless. I think about how the pendulum of life swings back and forth eternally, but our life on earth is merely a fleeting moment in the spectrum of time. I want to spend those moments in relief, in joy. I have to learn how to let go of my burden.

*Can I kiss you and try to make it better?*
*Can I hold you and embrace you with love to fade your fears?*
*How can I stop the bleeding of your wounded soul*
*When too many arrows have taken their toll?*
*I stood beside you in silence when you weren't strong,*
*When all of life's hurts had done you wrong.*
*I wanted to kiss you and make it better,*
*Because, love, I was there with you*
*Even when you didn't know it.*

# Premonitions

I dreamed I was in Las Vegas. My mother brushed up against me as she hurried toward the casino. Vegas was her favorite gambling venue, a place for her pleasures. She appeared as her younger beautiful self in her early fifties. Her stride was meaningful, her legs healthy, strutting forward with purpose. She stopped for a moment to look back, realizing it was me, her own daughter, whom she had just passed. I stood a couple of paces behind her on the sidewalk as her emerald green eyes glared at me, and a stabbing jolt of guilt overcame me. That familiar defiant gaze once again alerted me that she was angry because I had written a book and told people all about her. We shared no words, just that bone-chilling glare. My eyes met her gaze, surprised to see her, yet I could not speak.

\*\*\*

My sixth sense sometimes alerts me with dreams or a weird fluttering sensation in my stomach. This doesn't happen often, but when it does, I'm filled with an overwhelming anxiety in anticipation of what the sensation portends. As a superstitious person, I sometimes read too much into the meanings of things, but many times my premonitions are bang on. For instance, the first time my father had a heart attack, the butterflies were flying around inside me furiously, and something told me my dad was ill. Only moments later, my sister called to tell me the bad news. I had already dressed in anticipation of running somewhere once my feeling was confirmed.

I've had many of these occurrences throughout my life: inner warnings when something bad is about to happen.

*** 

The phone rang. It was Robby, calling to inform me that my mother was now living on borrowed hours, maybe a day or two. My emotions ran high, and I wrestled with them in a panic about how I would receive her death. As the hours passed, my heart sank a little further into that old abyss of guilt. I reprimanded myself for every moment I didn't go to her. Yet I didn't go.

Robby said she was no longer responsive at that point, and it conjured up visions of my dead father before he was buried, lying in his coffin. After learning how much my mother's appearance had deteriorated in the last few years of her life, I couldn't bear the thought of seeing her. I chose to remember my mother as the beauty she once had been. I knew that if I went to her side, she'd look at me with her icy stare and leave me with more hurtful parting words, whether spoken or implied, and I couldn't live with that.

After I hung up with Robby, I slumped onto the couch, and a few hours passed while I contemplated my guilt, conflicted at my decision not to go see my mother. I decided that the place I needed to be in that unsettled state of mind was my father's grave.

I often visit my father when something is troubling me. I feel a certain kind of peace when I'm there—odd for a girl who has always been afraid of cemeteries. When I visit him, I speak to my dad about current goings on in my life and update him on family matters. I always ask him to watch over my siblings and me, and sometimes I reminisce with him about funny times we shared. Eventually, a few tears well up from my heart, and I cry.

The day was sunny and still unseasonably warm for late October. The trees were still despite a slight passing wind. While standing in front of Dad's grave, I couldn't help but stare at the empty grave beside his, the one with the invisible *Reserved* sign.

A few years before my father's passing, he'd purchased an adjoining plot for my mother so she'd one day be laid to rest beside him. He was determined that if he couldn't have her in life on earth, he could at least have her in eternity. By that time, they'd been divorced for well over a decade, but that didn't deter him from remaining helplessly in love with her. They had managed to become friends, at least, a thread of something he could hang on to as she remained in his life.

Perhaps my mother found an ounce of compassion for the lost soul my father had become after having broken his heart too many times over the years. Nonetheless, she managed to use the friendship as an opportunity to manipulate him and extract money from him. He just could never say no to her.

Every time I visited my dad and found myself gazing upon that empty plot beside him, I wondered how he had remained mesmerized by a woman who had scorned him so many times in his young life. It baffled me that such a mild-mannered man could have hooked up with such a conniving person. As a child, I heard stories of such relationships all the time, but I never imagined my parents would live out those stories.

I couldn't help but lecture Dad. I must have repeated the same phrase to him umpteen times: "Were you crazy? She made your life a living hell. Didn't you suffer enough? Now you want to disturb your peace and spend eternity with her. What were you thinking?"

I wished I could have heard his response. Where he now resides, in another realm, does he regret his decision after watching the years of anguish my mother caused her children, or has his repeated forgiveness kept him stubbornly awaiting her arrival?

I told my father I had come to inform him that the moment my mother would join him was drawing near. The sky filled with clouds, and the surrounding maple trees began to sway as a sudden gust of wind swept across the cemetery. My gaze focused on a single leaf that had fallen off a nearby tree, and I watched as it danced around his headstone and landed on his grave. Then God released a flow of tears from the sky.

The beating rain and the swish of the windshield wipers kept rhythm as I drove home from the cemetery in deep contemplation. The radio playing in the background was barely audible, and it may as well have been off, as my ears were deaf with thoughts of my mother's demise. When I returned home, oddly enough, the sun had returned. I wondered whether that was a sign from

Dad letting me know it was okay with him. He could handle her from the other side.

# Drowning

My head bobbed up and down for what seemed like hours as I gasped for air in a deep, dark lagoon. I was alone in an unfamiliar place. I was drowning.

The nightmare continued throughout the night. It didn't matter how many times I woke, startled, with beads of sweat sticking to my brow. Every time I fell back asleep, I went back to that black lagoon.

The chill wouldn't leave me. The iciness left me numb, yet I managed to keep afloat, treading water. Neither the blankets nor my flannel nightshirt could stave off the cold stirring within me as I awoke each time throughout the night. I could feel a presence as though a cold spirit was exhaling its glacial breath in my bedroom.

I staggered out of bed early the next morning after a restless night. It was slightly past six thirty. After fighting to stay alive in the black lagoon, my inner knowing told me my mother was in transit to the next world. It was only a matter of time until I received the call from Robby to confirm my feelings. My mother was dying, and despite the years of our separation, I could still feel her spirit.

My heart jumped like a jack-in-the-box when the phone rang slightly after seven. It was startling yet expected. I glanced at the call display before clicking the answer button. Robby's number had appeared, confirming my suspicion.

My body fell limp upon hearing my brother, calm and somber, say, "Mom passed."

A million emotions danced through me in that moment. After my long silence while trying to hold back tears, I managed to speak through my shock. The finality of it hit me hard: My mother was dead. Even though I had known it was coming and had thought I was prepared for what I'd feel, I hadn't been. I offered to meet Robby at the funeral home to help him make arrangements. He tried to dissuade me from coming, stating almost heroically that it wasn't necessary, he could handle it.

I wasn't sure if Robby's comment was genuine or contained some resentment, subtly letting me know that he'd looked after everything else for my mother for years, so my services weren't required. However, I insisted I would meet him later that day after the doctor issued a death certificate and her body was picked up by the funeral home.

After I hung up, I stood for a moment like a statue frozen in time. My legs were paralyzed from shock as though nailed to the floor, and I couldn't speak as I absorbed the reality that my mother was dead. After a few moments passed, a wail of torturous pain rose from my soul. In my howling grief, I dropped to the floor in broken pieces. I was inconsolable. My mother was dead. After all the years wondering how I'd react to her death, I had never imagined the insurmountable hurt that flowed through my being.

My harrowing howls continued for another half hour before I was empty of sound and laden with grief.

\*\*\*

The chill wouldn't leave my body. I managed to get up off the floor, wrap myself in a blanket, and drag my rubbery legs downstairs to plop on the couch. The temperature outside was mild for an autumn day, and as I sat staring blankly into the glowing embers of the fireplace, I shivered.

The ice in my soul had yet to thaw as I struggled with myself for not having gone to sit with Robby while he waited for our mother to exit this world—and for not having gone to say goodbye. Once I had thought I was a good daughter, but now I was beginning to doubt myself. I foolishly thought

I had released all my pent-up angst while my mother lived.

*Tick tock* went the minutes. I couldn't seem to pry myself off the couch. No TV, no radio. Only the humming of the refrigerator and the crackling of the fire reminded me of my existence in those moments. My mind was busy revisiting pieces of my life.

Every so often, I picked up a pen and wrote down the fleeting thoughts I felt were important in those moments. I wasn't sure if I'd want to remember all of it later, but I needed to capture every changing emotion my mind experienced just in case.

*I feel lifeless.*
*I miss you, Mama.*
*I miss everything I didn't have from you.*
*Still, I am sorry.*
*I forgive you.*

# Regrets

I still think of my mother often. She's gone now but not forgotten. While she was still living, I wondered how I'd feel when she was gone. Would I feel relieved of my own self-imposed burden? Would I regret that she had left while we were no longer speaking?

My feelings are still a mixed bag. My guilty conscience plays on my empathy sometimes, and in those moments I question myself, wondering if I failed her. I remembered feeling much the same way when it was my responsibility to look after my siblings and father when I was young. I was conditioned to be the caretaker. I couldn't help but feel it was my duty to repair the broken state of my mother. My need to make her better, make us better, gnawed away at me for most of my life.

I couldn't accept that her temperament was beyond my control, and I didn't understand the complexities of dealing with a narcissist. I didn't even realize she was one until I was well into my twenties. I never intended to hurt her, no matter how deserving I felt she was of hurting many times. As fate would have it, she wound up hurting herself in the end, enduring estrangement from her loved ones with loneliness and suffering.

Mother had spent her lifetime hurting others with her wicked ways and lies, and I wish I could have known if she did so with intent to hurt or if she even realized how she treated people, if she truly believed her own lies. That question lingered in my mind for decades. Did she truly believe she was a good mother? Was she so lost in her imagined self and ego that she believed the things she said, or did she just know how to play the games and choose to live in her denial? The answers to those questions burn within me.

A veil of melancholia came over me every time I thought of my mother. As an empathetic person, I was used to putting myself in her lonely situation as she began to age and fell ill. I watched her with pity as she tried desperately to maintain her imagined noble status as her looks and body began to dissipate. I wished I could hug her and tell her it was okay to step down from her pedestal, as even a princess grows old and weary, but I couldn't. I didn't feel comfortable offering her affection. I wasn't used to it, and I wasn't certain how it would be received after so many failed attempts to console her in the past. I feared being told again that she didn't need anybody, that nobody cared about her anyway—the usual martyrdom. I could never win with my mother.

She didn't let her guard down often, but when she'd cry, whether for dramatic effect or genuinely, and it was difficult to distinguish between the two, it hurt my heart. I didn't want to see her cry. I didn't want her to show me her vulnerability because I didn't know how to comfort her. I felt powerless around her in good times and sad.

One memory in particular remains an albatross in my heart. When I was given the frightening diagnosis of a tumor on my heart valve and was told I would need open-heart surgery to remove it, the news was almost too much for me to bear. The day after receiving it, I realized I had to share it with my mother. She was entitled to hear it from me. This happened about a year and a half before I eventually had the final falling out with her, and I had yet to banish my mother from my life completely.

By that time in 2006, my mother was spending most of her time in bed or on the couch. She wore an oxygen mask and could still walk, albeit with a shaky stride, from the neuropathy in her legs due to the veins that had been taken out for her prior two open-heart surgeries. She was barely sixty-five but had suffered with congenital heart disease since her mid-fifties. As her illness consumed her and faded her beauty, her bitterness for what her life had become escalated. She often directed her fits of anger and displeasure at me as though I had smote her with her illness.

Despite my apprehension whenever I visited her, I decided that I should go to break my bad news to her in person. My frightened state of mind after learning about my own potential demise made the situation twice as uncomfortable for me.

After I explained my diagnosis, my mother appeared to be genuinely concerned. It was difficult for her to top that news, a practice she often used if someone shared something terrible with her. Instead of offering sympathy, she'd be only too glad to tell people why her situation was worse. But that day she didn't attempt to one-up me. Instead, lying propped up by pillows on her bed, Mother invited me to lie beside her so she could cuddle me.

In that moment, a whirlwind of emotions stormed through my head. I was thinking about my upcoming surgery. I was afraid I was going to die, and the last place I wanted to be at that time was with my mother. At first I felt sad at having to tell my mother the scary news. Then I began to feel resentful that just because I was about to have major surgery, I had been invited into her bed. The moment was overwhelming. I didn't know how to deal with the wave of confliction within me, so I told her I had to leave. I needed to get going and get my affairs in order in preparation for the surgery, just in case.

That is the saddest day I remember spending with my mother. I denied her wish to comfort her daughter as she lay in her sick bed. Until this very day, I remember those moments, and it hurts my soul that I didn't allow her to cradle me. I'm still not sure if it was because I felt she was undeserving of affection, resenting her offer because she'd never had the time of day for me before, or because I was so focused on getting out of her apartment and was feeling the clock ticking on my life. Whatever my unresolved reasons were that day, I regret that I didn't let her hold me in her own possible need for comfort as a mother whose child was seriously ill. I was beyond needing a mother's love by that time in our relationship. The awkwardness I felt in her presence was compounded by my own fears.

# Unspoken Words: In Apology

I know she had to have loved me in some misguided way, but my mother was always so busy being angry and vengeful about everything and everyone that I think she couldn't find the place inside her where love once must have resided.

I longed to have my mother's love, true, sincere, caring love, but I was never comfortable asking for it. The words *I love you* weren't familiar to me. The only times I recall her speaking them was when she'd been in one of her drunken or Valium-induced stupors, and then they sounded more like a cry for help.

I wished I could have shared with my mother that I knew how broken she was, but I also knew she'd never tolerate hearing that truth. It was painful for me not to be able to say what was in my heart. I wondered if it was painful for her too.

I had danced around her moods and whims all of my life, trying to appease her, wanting to be a good daughter. I wished she'd apologize to me just once for any of the many hurts she inflicted on me. *I'm sorry I threatened you all your life. I'm sorry I neglected you and wasn't a good mother. I'm sorry I played you as a pawn and used you as a weapon against your father. I'm sorry I wasn't there to answer your questions about life and womanhood. I'm sorry I forgot to congratulate you for any of your accomplishments. I'm sorry I had no interest in your school life, your prom, and your first heartbreak.* But there were no apologies.

Well, I'm sorry, Mom, for not confronting you and calling you out to your face for all the wrong things you did until I found the nerve much later in my life. And I'm sorry there was nothing I could do for you to make you happy. Instead, you shot me down with your sharp tongue, as you felt you had to belittle me for trying to help you. You always had the same response when I offered advice about your complaints, because you were afraid that maybe I knew something more than you did. Your standard response, "You think you're so fucking smart and have all the answers," was not comforting.

I'm sorry I couldn't say or do anything that made you happy. I'm sorry we didn't have a mother–daughter bond. Lord knows I tried many times to make things good with us, but you persisted to slap away the hand that reached out to you.

I'm sorry I couldn't bring myself to visit your bedside in your last hours. I couldn't handle rejection one more time. I'll remember your face as the beauty queen you once were. I didn't wish to say goodbye to you only for your hatred to be the last thing I could remember you by. I want to say I love you, yet it sounds so foreign to me.

I hold much love and compassion for the soul you kept hidden with hurt all of your life, the frightened, tormented little girl you kept encapsulated within yourself. The vulnerable part of you that you dared never to expose, I know it was there. That was the part of you I longed to know, the part I thought I could repair. But I couldn't.

I'm sorry.

# Broken Remains

Once upon a time, we were young and united. My siblings and I shared the same fear of our mother. If one of us were to receive her wrath, we all supported one another. We've all suffered her words and harbored them in our own ways—residual damage.

Now that my mother had left this earth, we were all facing a barrage of emotions. Guilt doesn't subside; it resides in the hidden nooks and crannies of our hearts.

Mel and I were grieving for the mother we felt we'd never had. Robby was a good son, waiting at our mother's side for her to go in peace, harboring his own secret sadness and wounds. Rory was in Europe on a cruise ship when our mother died. He had told Mel and me that he'd be fine if our mother passed while he was away, and he also isn't one to rehash the past. He had buried our mother years before in his mind—or so he said. I called bullshit. I know Rory well. He was the brother

I had first grown up with, fourteen months younger than me. It had taken him years to get over the passing of our father, and sometimes I have to wonder if he ever did.

My mother did some unforgivable things to Rory, so I know his hurt was deeply rooted. Our mother didn't spare any of us from hurt throughout our lives. Whether we've forgiven her or buried our pain, we never forget our wounds. They lie dormant and resurface in mysterious ways in our characters, mannerisms, and tolerances.

Throughout our lives, we four children had jumped to our mother's commands and endured her psychological warfare. Her specialty was pitting us against one another. She derived pleasure from badmouthing each of us to the others, thinking she was creating a secret bond. We'd all gone many rounds of not speaking to our mother. In our earlier adult years, we had tolerated her antics and the onslaught of guilt if something wasn't to her approval, but as the years passed, Mel and Rory had learned to stand up to our mother more vocally than Robby or I ever could. It took the final drops of emotional abuse to get me to follow in Rory and Mel's footsteps and finally walk away. Even with Robby being the only one left to attend to my mother's needs, he too eventually learned how to put her in her place.

With all the wars of words and our many exits in and out of our mother's life, she never failed to ask the same rhetorical question when she sensed our silent disapproval of her behavior: "Wasn't I a good mother?" It was her pity plea, the old *Woe is me*, and it grew tiring.

That question still haunts me. I have asked my siblings repeatedly through the years if our mother honestly believed she never did anything wrong or if that question was simply part of her award-winning performance. I wondered whether she felt guilty for her shortcomings as a mother. Either way, I found it pathetic when she asked, and all of us somehow managed to avoid replying. None of us wanted to hurt her by giving the answer she must have known deep inside her ego. One would think that after decades of posing the same question with no reply, she would stop asking, but she didn't. Anyone who knew my mother well knew better than to answer with the truth, because she was incapable of accepting it.

In the days when we were speaking, even though silence often prevailed between us, she'd occasionally ask me, "Was I such a terrible mother?" I never had the heart or the courage to reply with a yes. I didn't want to hurt her or bring her to tears, whether they were genuine or of the crocodile variety.

If one of us happened to not be on speaking terms with our mother and some time had passed, she'd use an excuse to pop back into our lives. This was her method of reconnecting without having to apologize for whatever had initially caused the rift. As the pattern repeated throughout the decades, we wound up letting her back into our lives many times because doing so was easier than confronting her with the issue of concern. We all knew we were never going to win an argument with her.

Our birthdays were particular dates she'd use to get back in our good graces. After all, how could a child ignore her mother when she called to say happy birthday?

\*\*\*

It was my forty-eighth birthday, June 7, 2007. In past years, my mother would call me first thing in the morning. Whether we had been on speaking terms or not when my birthday arrived, she'd take the liberty of calling me, using it as a great excuse to get her foot back in the door of my life—a good icebreaker.

But this morning was different. Despite the lack of a call, I couldn't put to rest my nagging feelings of dread that my mother would once again use my birthday to try to re-enter my life. My anxiety about the possibility had nothing to do with what I would say to her, as I had made a final and clear break from her in the previous fall of 2006, and I didn't intend to answer the phone if she dared call me. I wasn't going to be forced to repeat the past. Even so, my butterflies were churning with concern about how terrible I'd feel for her if she called and I refused to answer.

My nerves had the best of me all day. The morning passed, but I was afraid that perhaps she was summoning the courage to call later. Nervously, I checked the call display each time the phone rang, but the day also passed with no attempts from my mother. I knew then that the finality had set in with her: We were broken beyond repair.

This was the first birthday in my life that she didn't call me. I wept not because she didn't call but because my empathy for her had gotten the best of me. She knew she didn't have any more tricks in her bag to bring back a daughter whose feelings she had wounded for the last time. I knew she couldn't have forgotten it was my birthday, and I wondered if somewhere in her empty soul, my mother was grieving the loss of another child.

After the day ended, I came to terms with myself. I was proud of my resolve in keeping with my decision not to allow my mother back into my life.

***

July was my mother's birthday. Somehow, my guilt eased when I didn't call her on her birthday either. My birthday had been a test of my commitment to keeping my mother out of my life. It helped me that June came before July. Had my mother's birthday come before mine after our final falling out, I think it would have destroyed me not to acknowledge it no matter our status. Her failing to acknowledge my birthday first had been a relief.

# Facts and Fiction

My childhood was definitely no fairy tale. In fact, it wasn't much of a childhood at all. My mother wasn't present for much of it, busy with her friends, traveling, and building up her social status. My parents' marriage was doomed before it began.

I was seven when I began questioning my father about the year he and my mother were married. The math didn't add up, and my question became an unanswered riddle until I was old enough to figure things out on my own and get some verification from my aunts.

I was the means my mother had used to entrap my father. Her alluring beauty had him under a spell, but snaring my dad into marriage wasn't enough for her. She desired the attention of every man as well as materialistic things to embellish her status and show off to others. She put on her charming facade in public and manipulated people with her lies and grandiose stories. She was emotionally devoid of a mother's love, and she broke my father's heart many times over with her flaunting and flirting and countless indiscretions.

Not until I was well into my thirties did I discover many truths from lies. Aunty Lee confirmed the religious status of her mother, the truth of the planning of my conception, and the year my parents were married, yet my mother continued to deny the truth, grandly elaborating about her and my father being so in love that they couldn't wait to get married. According to her, they secretly wed when she was seventeen in 1957, and when she found out she was two months pregnant with me, they had another ceremony in November of 1958 to make it public knowledge and avoid the stigma of having a child out of wedlock. She remained adamant that I hadn't been conceived out of wedlock because they had been married the previous year.

That story wasn't sitting well with me. They were married but living apart? What made more sense was that my father was afraid to marry her because of his parents' disapproval, but once my mother got pregnant, the situation had to be re-evaluated. It was the norm back in that era: If you got a girl pregnant, you married her.

Incidentally, it wasn't much of a wedding. Other than my parents standing up before a rabbi for the service, there was no grand celebration. I also learned my father's parents weren't present. My mother had lost her own mother four years prior when she died from a stroke after a car crash. I suppose just her father and siblings may have been present. It was no wonder that when I asked her as a child to tell me about her wedding, eager to hear about the romantic day my parents wed, she persisted in changing the subject. The fact that I had never seen one wedding picture was another indication that there was something to hide.

My mother gave birth to four children. All of us were accidents, starting with me, the deceptive intentional accident. Five months after my birth, she was pregnant with Rory. Undoubtedly, Rory was conceived from makeup sex shortly after my mother returned from abandoning me when I was barely a few months old. My father finding her and begging her to come back was the beginning of their cat and mouse marriage, which set the tone for many similar events to follow.

Rory didn't receive the same attention from my dad as I had. I think this hurt him very much as a child. My father was a gentle man, and as I got older and relived pieces of our childhood, I couldn't help but wonder if he harbored a lingering resentment for my mother's affair after my birth, causing a possible detachment from Rory. No matter how much he was obsessed with my mother, perhaps there would always be a seed of bitterness.

My parents separated numerous times, so we moved a lot. Whenever there was another breakup, my dad sold a house. Consequently, when they reunited, we moved again. Their reunions never lasted longer than the time they actually spent apart. During one of our transitional apartment moves after another split, my dad once again begged my mother back, and Robby was conceived in that apartment.

There was a lot of chatter behind the walls regarding Robby's conception. I recall Aunty Lee telling me my mother had been having another affair, which had been the cause of that separation, but my father still came to visit us periodically while trying to win my mother's heart back. I vaguely remember waking up one night, going into my mother's room, and catching my parents in a compromising position during that separation. That very well might have been the night of Robby's conception.

Robby's angelic nature coupled with his piercing big blue eyes and albino white hair drew the affections of anyone surrounding him. Oddly enough, I never sensed any distance between my father and him. After Robby was born, my parents reunited, and we moved to a new house once again. A year and a half later, with plenty of discord in the household, my sister Melanie was conceived, and before she was two, my father had once again moved out.

Melanie was the last child born into our family, and she became an instant joy in Rory's life. He protected her from the day she was born. Within a year after Melanie's birth, my mother endured gynecological problems that eventually led to a hysterectomy. No more babies would be born. I wondered if God thought four were enough.

It didn't take me too long, once I reached my teen years, to realize I did not want to be like my mother at all.

When I was younger and asked my mother questions about her mother, I received candy-coated responses about what she chose to remember, her fantasized versions that made situations appear more wonderful than they were. Much controversy stemmed from my family's faith and religion. Only after my mother's death did more information about her family history come to light. Some of the mysterious dark secrets, held captive from us, were unraveled. Many of the falsehoods my mother had led us to believe began to take on clarity after I summoned the courage to get confirmations and explanations from Aunty Lee.

My mother had sometimes shared snippets of her childhood in passing conversation. In her true delusional style, her stories, spiced up for dramatic effect, were spun with a twist to invoke pity. Not to my surprise, I found out how warped those stories were. *What was the big deal?* I wondered. It wasn't like anyone had a criminal record, so why was it so difficult for my mother to admit the truth of her heritage? I couldn't understand why she couldn't tell a story without exaggerating. Everything she told us was sensationalized to attract praise or sympathy. Weren't we entitled to learn the truth about our family roots?

My mother's ongoing refusal to admit the truth about her mother's religion became a topic of conversation with my aunts and me through the years. The secret had come out long ago when two of my aunts confirmed that their mother wasn't Jewish, yet my mother lived in denial. I couldn't understand why. If she was denying the truth only to maintain her imagined golden reputation, whom was she fooling?

Why would it have been so terrible for her not to be Jewish? Would it have made her less desirable to society? Would it have been a blemish on her perfect picture of herself, making her unacceptable in the social circles she strived to become part of, the circles rich Jewish boys congregated in? Certainly, my father and his parents knew the truth. That was part of the reason my grandparents weren't happy with my father's choice of a bride.

My mother remained adamant about the fantasy in which her protestant mother from Scottish descent had converted to Judaism when she married my Jewish grandfather, but that was not the case. There never had been any conversion, and when my mother married my father, born to two emigrated Russian Orthodox Jews, her story wasn't received so well by my grandparents.

In Jewish law, you are what your mother is, so my mother wasn't considered Jewish, although she denied it all the way to her grave. The funniest part of all of this was that, pretend or not, she never practiced the religion. It boiled my grandparents' blood that their son wasn't raising traditional Jewish children.

My paternal grandparents frowned upon my mother's background, and I believe that even if her mother had converted, it still wouldn't have been enough to appease them. If the matter of religion wasn't enough to swallow, my mother's plan to get pregnant in order to snag my father was a disgrace to them. I was the one who had been conceived illegitimately to set the bait when my mother was eighteen, and consequently I didn't receive much attention or love from my grandparents. It was apparently my fault my father had married my mother.

Although my father's parents were old-fashioned, verbally inexpressive, and unemotional people, those traits didn't make them bad. However, as a child seeking affection from them and not receiving any, I resented them. I couldn't comprehend what I'd done wrong to deserve no love or affection, and when I turned eight, I came to realize how strained my grandparents' relationship was with my mother. Anyone could sense the forced niceties between them.

My mother often badmouthed my grandparents in our household, and at my young and impressionable age, I tended to side with her. I believed everything she told me. Why wouldn't I have? She was my mother, and those cronies were cold toward me. That was before I understood why my grandparents resented and harbored animosity for my mother.

As the years passed and I learned more about my mother and her conniving ways, I questioned whether I had been too harsh in judging my grandparents. Their reasons for not liking my mother were certainly justified, but I couldn't get past why they punished me for her behavior. I kept my feelings to myself when around them.

My mother's childhood wasn't ideal either. She was the youngest of six, left to fend for herself after her mother died. She grew up poor, and her mother had loved to gamble with whatever money there had been while she was alive. My maternal grandmother, Dorothy, was a feisty, party-loving beauty. She was an exotic, sensual woman projecting immense sex appeal, and her raven-black hair, sultry deep brown eyes, and robust personality had heads turning to admire her everywhere she went. In fact, she was a runner up in the first ever Miss Toronto Beauty Pageant.

I believe my mother adored her mother, captivated by her beauty and exuberance the same way I once was with hers when I was younger. As children, we tend to emulate people who fascinate us. When Grandmother Dorothy died, she left behind an impressionable child to grow up on her own. This had to have had some effect on my mother, who began building herself up in a Scarlett O'Hara sort of manner.

I truly believe her mother's death brought on the beginning of my mother's narcissistic disorder. She had her mother's looks, a dark beauty long before she changed her hair color to red, and she'd witnessed her mother's dominant personality and watched how her beauty had given her many advantages in winning her desires. I'm sure those factors were instrumental in my mother's decision to mimic what she knew, aiding in her plans to get what she wanted using her looks. Thus her ego grew with her into the person she became.

My mother was just an emotionally abandoned girl who had vowed she wouldn't be poor all her life and desperately wanted to taste the finer things. The only problem was that she got a little too full of herself and trampled people and their hearts along the way. Greed and jealousy were integral characteristics of her makeup and subsequently her downfall.

\*\*\*

Throughout the years when my siblings and I would get together and compare various versions of the bizarre stories my mother had told us, the wedding date debacle would come into the conversation, and we'd have a good laugh together over it. Then my sister-in-law Katie, Rory's wife, took interest in the riddle and decided to do some digging.

My fifty-sixth birthday fell during the mourning period, known in the Jewish faith as sitting shiva, for Aunty Lee eight months after my mother died. Katie, curious to learn more about our family lineage, had been working on our family tree, and after we ate dinner, she brought out a gluten-free chocolate birthday cake she had baked for me. She then handed me a present. When I opened the lovely gift bag and pulled out the pretty tissue paper, inside was an envelope containing a copy of my parents' marriage certificate. There it was in black and white: November 11, 1958. There was the proof, verified after so many lies. My mother had been two months pregnant with me when she got legally married, and there was no other record of marriage between my parents.

Attached to the certificate was a simple piece of paper with a handwritten note from Katie: *There is nothing better than knowing that you are legit.*

# Misleading Values

When I was a little girl, my mother drilled into me that I should be nice to my paternal grandparents even though they weren't affectionate to me so that they would keep me in their wills until they died. She wasn't concerned about the fact that I was unhappy every weekend I was shipped off to their house with my siblings in my childhood years so she could be free to gallivant as she pleased. She insisted that I do as I was told, leaving no room to bargain or explain my unhappiness.

I didn't think much about her advice because, as a child, I had yet to realize the power of money. As I grew older, I learned a lot about it and all the evils that came along with it.

Although I felt no emotion toward my grandparents, I kept my opinions about their lack of love for me to myself. I found it difficult to pretend to be nice to them when they had no interest in me. I was just grateful my siblings kept me company for the eternity of the weekends I endured at my grandparents' home for many years.

I never gave much thought to money when I was a kid. I just longed for acknowledgment and love. After watching my mother manipulate my father for whatever she could extract from him, I realized I wasn't going to kiss anybody's ass for anything or pretend to like anyone for personal gain. If my grandparents didn't like me, I didn't want their money.

My father's defeat and the repeated dashing of his hopes of being awarded with my mother's affections had taught me good lessons about using people for their money. I refused to take my mother's advice. I grew to learn that people had to respect one another to earn respect, and I wasn't a cold and calculating person like my mother, taking advantage of people and acting insincerely to acquire materialistic things.

An invisible wall had always existed between my grandparents and me, and I wasn't prepared to pretend I was a doting granddaughter just so I could win something from them in the end. I was fine in my resolve, and I still am. Some said my stubborn refusal to make nice would bite me back some day, but I was good with my decision. My stance absolved me from becoming like my mother.

In the end, I got what I deserved, which wasn't much at all, but I was okay with that. If I'd listened to my mother and pretended to be loving and attentive to my grandparents, begging to be loved, I might have been financially well off at the sacrifice of my conscience. In retrospect, I have my pride, and in not succumbing to lowly tactics out of greed, I feel better about myself.

It wasn't too often that my mother offered me words of wisdom or much in the way of motherly advice. She mostly spoke to glorify herself. Sadly, I can't say my mother ever told me anything of value. My lessons came from analyzing the things she did, and one thing was certain: Her footsteps were not the ones I chose to follow in life.

# Reconciliations

There's a difference between two people attempting to reconcile, discussing their differences with open minds in search of resolution from conflict, and one person reconciling the differences by herself. My mother did not afford me any opportunity to rehash our differences, because she was much too defensive to admit she'd ever done wrong. The few times I attempted to confront her about how she'd hurt me only seemed to stoke the fire in her. According to her, she had never said, done, or implied anything wrong, and her speeches always ended with "How dare you accuse me?" The reconciling I had with my mother was something I had to do within myself.

Getting my mother to admit her shortcomings was like expecting the sun to shine at midnight. It became much easier to ignore her than to try to have an open discussion together that could never result in anything positive. The only means she had to feel good about herself was demeaning others.

My mother loved to martyr herself to me about what a wonderful mother she was, how I was ungrateful to her for the invented things she told me she'd done for me. She would then take the opportunity to bash my siblings by telling me what useless pieces of shit they were, targeting a different one depending on the day. Those conversations came up when she didn't get her way with one of us. The strange part was that she never realized that my siblings and I later shared those delusional conversations among ourselves. It was as though she thought she was sharing a private confidence with one of us, that we were going to nod in agreement and keep it our little secret. Playing one child against the other was one of her favorite pastimes.

It came as no surprise that the sum of her life had left her with only two friends, her gambling chums. Years of her belittling, gloating, and lying to those in her circles had caused many to leave her. It seemed a pretty face could no longer shield the contents of the package.

Reconciling a broken relationship is difficult to do while boxed in with past perceptions. I knew I'd never be able to reconcile with my mother, so I had to do it for myself. I had to assess my anger and resentments and digest them before I could resolve them. When my mother wasn't willing to admit her wrongs for us to have a real reconciliation, I learned to accept that I had done my best to make amends, and instead I had to make peace with myself.

I knew from past attempts that overlooking my mother's flaws and allowing her back into my life would only lead to a repeat performance. I knew this because my mother never learned from her mistakes. She simply wouldn't own up to them. I could have done a thousand and one things for her, and the one time I had to tell her no, she wouldn't hesitate to tell me what a selfish person I was, that I never did anything for her. She had no regard for my life, my marriage, or my time. Trying to resolve issues with her only left more guilt from her denial of the situation in question, and she would spin the issue to reflect something I'd done to her, taking the blame off herself. That was her specialty, making us all feel guilty when confronted. I lived that way with her for most of my life, and neither I nor anyone else could change her. It took me a lifetime to learn that I had nothing to feel guilty for.

I'll never know what my mother really thought of our many futile reconciliations from the past. I still wonder if she thought everything was fine between us or if somewhere deep inside she knew there was no glue that could connect our broken pieces.

I came to terms in my heart with the fact that my mother was a troubled soul. It took me many years to let go of my hurt and resentment toward her by putting my feelings into perspective, realizing I'd done my best to appease her and keep the peace, but I wasn't responsible for her behavior. I finally realized I couldn't fix her. I can't change people, especially those who don't believe they've done anything wrong.

It becomes tiring to have to apologize to a wrongdoer. Countless times, I swallowed my hurt and pride to make peace only to receive no peace at all. It was only a matter of time before the next outburst of hurtful words would send me off in retreat. It's difficult to reconcile with someone who feels entitled to be in your life solely because she's your mother.

# The Funeral

The day after my mother died, we laid her body to rest in the grave that awaited her arrival. In our faith, we bury the dead the day after they die unless that day turns out to be the Sabbath or a holy day, in which case the burial takes place the following day.

My husband and I met up with my sister and her children at Robby's house, where the limousine waited to take us all to the funeral home for the service before going to the cemetery. The ambiance was somber, not much said among us. I suppose we were all deep in reflection. I felt as though a lifetime of conflict had been reduced to the final few hours of my mother's time left on earth as I fast forwarded and replayed our lives together in my mind.

Melanie had been in touch with Rory by text to keep him abreast of our plans. I was grateful that he was abroad on his Mediterranean cruise when our mother died, as I was concerned that if he had been home, he'd have been conflicted, wrestling with his decision not to be at her funeral or sit shiva for our customary mourning period.

As it turned out, my suspicions were not wrong. Rory too experienced an explosion of hurt rising within him and exiting his body when he realized our mother was no longer alive, and he went to the ship's chapel every morning to say the Kaddish, the prayer for the dead, for her soul. He had his own demons to deal with.

The funeral service was small but lovely. Before the service, the rabbi asked us children some questions about our mother's life so he could include some stories in his eulogy. That was a difficult discussion and a rather depressing moment. We didn't want to tell flowery lies, but neither did we want to send our mother off with any bitterness. He asked us about things she enjoyed in her life, and ultimately we shared with him her passion for gambling and a few short remembrances of our "fun" summers in Fort Erie during our childhood years. We kept out the reason why we went to Fort Erie and the babysitter who came along with us so our mother could go to the racetrack every day and party at night.

The rabbi's speech was short and sweet. He said the usual prayers and talked about things related to death in the Torah, and he put a fun sort of spin on our childhood memories. Certain phrases he used, such as *good mother* and the translation of my mother's Hebrew name, which was a true oxymoron, had me flinching as I sat listening. But I let it pass. I allowed my mother her moment.

Although filled with conflicting emotions, I can't recall shedding many tears. I had already exhausted myself the day before when I found out she died. But when my eldest niece, Melanie's daughter, stepped up to the podium to read an ode she'd written for her grandmother, the waterworks were once again ignited. My heart was touched with the sad reminder that my niece had grown older and her grandmother hadn't been much of a presence in her life. She too had taken her share of verbal licks through her adolescence since Melanie had banished our mother and no longer stuck around to take them. But my niece, who knew of all the grief in our lives courtesy of our mother, still remembered the times in her younger life when her grandmother had been nice to her. I didn't cry for my loss. I cried for the little girl who had gotten caught in the crossfire between her mother and grandmother and had inherited the venom meant for Melanie.

I turned my head in curiosity to scan the chapel and see how many people had shown up for the service. There wasn't much of a crowd: my siblings and their children, me and my husband, a few cousins, Aunty Lee, a few close friends of mine and my siblings, and two friends of my mother. It was a rather compact crowd to honor a grandiose life.

After the service, we returned to the limo and headed to the cemetery. A stabbing sadness panged my heart as I watched Robby, his son, and our nephews, Mel's boys, carry their mother and grandmother to her final resting place below the soil. Reality had set in. It was the end of an era, a broken legacy.

The rabbi read off the prayers and blessings for the dead, and we lined up to take turns at the shovel, where we all paid our last respects by throwing some dirt on the casket as part of the burial tradition. There were no loud sobs to speak of, although there were some glassy eyes and looks of contemplation from Robby, Mel, and me. While people continued to pay their last respects with the shovel, I peeked to my side, slightly raising my sunglasses to check on my family, and I caught a glimpse of Aunty Lee weeping for her last remaining sibling.

My heart felt heavy and dark even though the sun was shining. I stared at my father's grave, hoping for a sign of his content, but the winds were silent.

# Things We Keep

We sat shiva for three days at Robby's house. During that time, our friends and family came to visit and pay their respects. I felt as though some of the broken threads among Robby, Mel, and me were mending. We had plenty of time to talk, allowing us all to strengthen some of our tattered feelings. We reminisced about some of our childhood memories, good and bad, and Robby's wife, Reena, brought up a box of old pictures she'd kept in storage in her basement from my mother's apartment.

Various other boxes lay scattered in the back corner of the living room. Those contained all that remained of my mother. Her once grand life filled with beautiful clothes, shoes, and jewels which had long since been pawned for gambling money had been reduced to a few boxes of worn pajamas, a couple of bathrobes, a few faded sweatshirts, and two old blankets. Only the essentials remained, things sick people wear to feel comfortable and warm.

I stood for a moment, focused on the boxes. The reminder of my mother's loneliness and all she had left in the world was painful to digest. The guilt once again rose within me. I knew the outcome of her life wasn't my fault, yet my heart in that moment was punishing me for her lonely existence.

Reena asked Mel and me if we wanted anything from the boxes before she donated the items to charity. I couldn't bring myself to want anything, and I shivered at the thought of keeping any part of my mother's shattered life in my possession.

Later, while we sat back on the couch in our mourner seats, Mel and I looked over the box of photos. My mother was not much of a camera buff, and many of the photos she'd accumulated through the years had been taken by others and given to her, mostly of family milestones and celebrations. There were various pictures, a few photos from Robby's wedding and of her grandchildren. There were no photos of Melanie, Rory, or me. They seemed to have vanished. Aunty Lee wore a shameful look as she told me she'd watched my mother tear them up and throw them away a few years back.

I looked at some old photos buried at the bottom of the box. The faded images in those photos reminded me of my childhood, my dead aunts and uncles, and my mother. Then there was one letter.

While I was in Greece in my mid-twenties, I called my father several times, but I also sent a few letters to my mother. It was difficult to reach her by phone with the time difference, and being that she was barely ever home, it was just easier to drop her a line in writing.

The letter was still intact, neatly tucked into its original envelope. I was shocked to find she had kept it through the decades. I was sure she must have overlooked it while she went into her phase of destroying photos, probably not even realizing it remained. In the letter, I sounded like my jovial self, giving her a detailed account of the places I'd visited and sharing some of the fascinating experiences I'd had touring the Greek islands. I sounded like a Fodor travel writer. There was nothing mushy in the letter. It was more or less an informative hello mentioning some things I missed back home, mostly the conveniences of modern appliances.

Mother never replied to any of my letters. This didn't faze me at the time because that was her standard behavior, but I would love to know whether she saved that one letter or it was an oversight in her clearing.

# The Stone

I t is customary in our faith to put up a headstone on the grave of a lost loved one within one year of his or her death. Once the stone is erected, we have a small ceremony of prayers at the graveside known as the unveiling. A white muslin cloth remains tied around the stone to cover the inscription until the ceremony begins, when it is cut off by the rabbi before the prayers for the dead.

Fall of 2014 passed, as did winter and spring of the following year. Robby called me to discuss plans for having the stone cut and engraved for our mother. He informed me that he knew a place that made the stones, but we needed to discuss the details of the design—and the wording.

A few days later, he sent me a scanned photo of a preliminary drawing of the stone as well as a photo of my father's headstone. The designer pointed out that since my parents' graves were side by side, they should match in design with the exception of the Star of David on my dad's stone and a menorah on my mother's. The stonecutter also advised that the wording on both stones should be similar. This presented a huge dilemma for Robby and me.

As I read the proposed wording on the photo, I remembered the heart-wrenching day I buried my father. Worse, I couldn't accept putting those same words on my mother's stone. I just couldn't fathom the idea of the same heartfelt loving words I had chosen for my father being engraved on my mother's headstone. I battled my thoughts, wondering how two stones could say the same thing for two entirely different souls. I was fine about the two stones matching in design, but the wording plagued me with concern.

My father's stone included the words *Beloved husband and devoted father.* The template of the stone Robby had sent me omitted the descriptive words, yet he had penciled them in with question marks as though to ask me, *What should we say?*

I sat in silence for a few moments while past hurts resurfaced within me. I struggled with my emotions. What would be the proper thing to do? I didn't hate my mother, yet I couldn't put lies on her stone. I refused to be a hypocrite and use words such as *devoted mother*, and I was torn with indecision as to what was appropriate for a monument to stand for all eternity, for the public to see, for us four not to be judged upon, and that would allow her some dignity.

Robby and I discussed our dilemma. We both felt the same about the situation, hence the question marks on the template. Neither of us wanted to air our laundry publicly. Neither Robby nor I was cold or callous. The process of deciding what to write was a painful one.

I continued to look at the wording on my dad's stone while chatting and sharing thoughts with Robby on the phone. I scribbled some alternate words on a scrap of paper in hopes of capturing a feeling that sat well with me and was appropriate for the stone. It was imperative we found the right words. The words had to demonstrate some sort of tribute to our mother, something succinct and truthful, but we also had to feel comfortable in our own skin with what we chose.

Robby and I finally agreed that *In loving memory* would be engraved across the header, just as it had been on our father's stone. After much deliberation, we chose to allow the word *beloved* before *wife* because, after all, our mother was our father's beloved. We omitted the word *devoted* because it felt like a blatant dishonesty to ourselves and to anyone who'd read it, knowing the story of us. We agreed on *Loving mother and grandmother* to replace it, as we saw the word *loving* as having several connotations.

My concept of the word denoted that some hidden part of my mother's soul did love her children. We also knew that despite her lack of participation in our lives, she'd been a better grandmother than she ever had been a mother. And so it was written.

# Forgiveness

Forgiveness is a process. I couldn't simply offer forgiveness until I processed my hurts and inflictions.

A person committing a hurt may not always be deserving of forgiveness, but if we can find that place of forgiveness in our hearts, it cleanses us. It's nice to think wrongdoers can have remorse, take responsibility for their own actions, and apologize, but some people choose to deny their misbehaviors and are consequently incapable of asking for or accepting forgiveness. In those instances, such as in the relationship I had with my mother, it became up to me to forgive her without seeking her remorse and without her even knowing. I did this to release my own internal burden.

It was healthier for me to make peace with myself by forgiving my mother. Carrying and relentlessly trying to swallow a lifetime of hurt while hoping to no avail that my mother would come to her senses and acknowledge her misconduct had led me to understand her inability to apologize for things she didn't believe she was guilty of doing. I decided not to carry the blame any longer for being an absent daughter. It was only with the passage of time that I learned I couldn't change her and that I was not a bad person for choosing to sever ties.

I didn't just decide to let go of our relationship. I fought my own advice and kept trying to make it better. Only once I was certain in my soul that I'd made the best effort to reconcile more times than I probably should have did I learn to let go and free myself in forgiveness. It takes two willing people to reconcile, and realizing my mother wasn't willing, I had to find that closure within myself.

I never verbally offered my forgiveness to my mother because it would have proved futile. She believed she was perfect, so in her mind there was nothing to be forgiven for. It was up to me to find my own peace.

After all my years of jumping at her commands and resenting her, I had never told her how I felt except for that one final blow I delivered to her when I banished her forever from my life. However, as I witnessed her decline from her imagined state of greatness to a lonely, sick woman and tried to figure out why she was who she was, my pity for her intensified. I had already surpassed the hurtful times, and there was nothing positive about hanging on to them. I felt sorry for what had become of my mother's life, and I found a place in my heart to forgive her for behaviors I truly believe were caused by her mental narcissistic illness. She never knew any better. I realized I couldn't repair a mother who didn't believe she was broken—but there was still a chance for me to heal.

I forgave her because I didn't want to hate her, and I didn't want her to leave this earth without my having let God know I'd found a way to understand and forgive her. So I set her free of her sins, and in turn I set myself free.

Ending a relationship is, in a sense, like a death, a final parting of ways. It evokes many of the same emotions and stages as does grieving. I had to go through anger, questioning my convictions, and coming to a realization when I knew and accepted I had done everything in my power to rectify my broken relationship with my mother. I had to reach a final tipping point of not being able to take one more ounce of pain before I realized there was no going back, but by no means did my decision to leave my mother lessen the compassion I had for her.

In the end, my wounded soul accumulated a lifetime of lessons and a new acceptance of forgiveness for both my mother and myself. I will never forget the hardships I endured as a child and throughout my life with my mother, slighted with emotional neglect and tortured by guilt, but I forgave myself for abandoning her and for the mountain of guilt I had let myself hold on to just because I believed I had to honor my parent. After almost half a century of enduring emotional abuse, I had served my time and allowed myself to let go.

I cannot change or forget the past, but with new understanding I can move forward with a heart less heavy.

*I forgive you, Mother.*

# Epilogue

We don't get to choose our families. However, although nobody's life is perfect, there are standards for what constitutes good parenting and a normal childhood. Those standards may not have applied in my upbringing, but I never let my past sway me to believing that my mother's actions were justified. How she chose to go through life was a pattern I was determined not to repeat. I learned from her mistakes. Happiness and healthy relationships aren't created by using and hurting others to acquire our desires.

I made a life for myself despite my internal damage. I found my place in the world. I triumphed, albeit with some mistakes, and formed successful relationships, friendships, and a marriage. I have had several careers and have become a published author despite never having learned anything of value from my upbringing. I chose my own path, and perhaps my biggest mistake was waiting for so many years to allow myself to let go of the guilt that consumed me, the guilt I harbored for walking away from my mother.

I've come a long way from that scared little girl. I experienced firsthand how disrespect in a relationship, parental or marital, does not allow growth and love to flourish. I learned how selfishness and self-centeredness ultimately turn into loneliness in the end, and I learned that no matter how much I have thought at times in my life that I needed a mother, that was more a desire for something I thought I was entitled to than a true need. As it turned out, I didn't need my mother at all. I managed to find my own way to happiness.

Society dictates what we need, but blood or no blood, if a parent isn't nurturing and has no regard for a child's feelings and wellbeing or causes her ongoing anguish, it's time to leave. I might have stayed too long, but I eventually learned to give myself permission to let go.

# End

Thank you for reading *P.S. I Forgive You.* If you enjoyed this book, please consider telling your friends and posting a short review by going to my author page on Amazon at:

www.amazon.com/author/dgkaye7

Click on the book cover and the "Write a review" box. Word of mouth is an author's best friend and is much appreciated.

# About the Author

D.G. Kaye is a Canadian author living in Toronto. She is a nonfiction writer of memoirs about her life experiences, matters of the heart, and women's issues. Her positive outlook keeps her on track, allowing her to take on life's challenges with a dose of humor and a mission to overcome adversity.

D.G. began writing when pen and paper became the tools to express her pent-up emotions during her turbulent childhood. She began journaling about her life at a young age and continued writing about the people and events that left imprints and lessons. She writes books to share her stories and inspiration.

D.G. is a big advocate for kindness and for empowering women. Her favorite saying is "For every kindness, there should be kindness in return. Wouldn't that just make the world right?"

When she's not writing, D.G. loves to read (self-help books and stories of triumph), cook (concocting new recipes, never to come out the same way twice), shop (only if it's a great sale), play poker (when she gets the chance), and, most of all, travel.

Visit her website at www.dgkayewriter.com and join her mailing list to keep up with her latest blogs and news about her books and events.

Contact D.G. at author@dgkayewriter.com.

## Follow D.G. on her social sites:
www.twitter.com/@pokercubster
www.facebook.com/dgkaye
www.linkedin.com/in/dgkaye7
www.google.com/+DebbyDGKayeGies
www.pinterest.com/dgkaye7
www.instagram.com/dgkaye

**Visit D.G.'s author page:**
www.amazon.com/author/dgkaye7.
www.goodreads.com/dgkaye

# Other Books by D.G. Kaye

## *Conflicted Hearts*
*A Daughter's Quest for Solace from Emotional Guilt*
Purchase link:
www.smarturl.it/bookconflictedhearts

*"Somehow I believed it was my obligation to try to do the right thing by her because she had given birth to me."*

Burdened with constant worry for her father and the guilt caused by her mother's narcissism, D.G. Kaye had a short childhood. When she moved away from home at eighteen, she began to grow into herself, overcoming her lack of guidance and her insecurities.

Her life experiences became her teachers, and she learned from the mistakes and choices she made along the way, plagued by the guilt she carried for her mother.

*Conflicted Hearts* is a heartfelt journey of self-discovery and acceptance, an exploration of the quest for solace from emotional guilt.

## Excerpt: Tit for Tat

Their argument seemed vague to me, but it had sent my mother out of the house in a flurry. I was three, and we were living in our first house on Homewood Avenue, a pretty place with a big red oak tree on the front lawn. Even at three, I loved that house, our first family home.

It was nightfall. I had just finished helping my dad change my baby brother's diaper, Rory being one and a half years old. My dad went into the kitchen and emptied a drawer of its contents, placing the butter knives in a container. He asked me to come help him, and we went into the front vestibule, where I held the container of knives as he drew his hammer. I handed him the knives one by one as I curiously watched him insert them between the door and the jamb all around the doorframe.

I asked him, "What are we doing, Daddy?"

Pounding his hammer against the base of a knife, he replied, "We're locking Mommy out in case she tries to come home."

I didn't know this wasn't a common practice. I thought it was just something one did in response to an argument—it had been part of my conditioning to accept this as normal behavior. It wasn't long after this event that Dad sold our beautiful home with the red oak tree and we ended up moving to a little apartment on Bathurst Street without him.

# *Words We Carry*
## *Essays of Obsession and Self-Esteem*
Purchase link: www.smarturl.it/bookwordswecarry

*"I have been a great critic of myself for most of my life, and I was darned good at it, deflating my own ego without the help of anyone else."*

What do our shopping habits, high-heeled shoes, and big hair have to do with how we perceive ourselves? Do the slights we endured when we were young affect how we choose our relationships now? D.G. takes us on a journey, unlocking the hurts of the past by identifying situations that hindered her own self-esteem. Her anecdotes and confessions demonstrate how the hurtful events in our lives linger and set the tone for how we value our own self-worth. *Words We Carry* is a raw, personal accounting of how the author overcame the demons of low self-esteem with the determination to learn to love herself.

### *MenoWhat? A Memoir*
### *Memorable Moments of Menopause*
Purchase ink:
www.smarturl.it/bookMenoWhatAMemoir

*"I often found myself drifting from a state of normal in a sudden twist of bitchiness."*

From PMS to menopause to what the hell?

D.G. adds a touch of humor to a tale about a not-so-humorous time. While bidding farewell to her dearly departing estrogen, D.G. struggles to tame her raging hormones of fire, relentless dryness, flooding and droughts and other unflattering symptoms.

Join D.G. on her meno-journey to slay the dragons of menopause as she tries to hold on to her sanity, memory, hair, and so much more!

### *Have Bags, Will Travel*
### *Trips and Tales: Memoirs of an Over-packer*
Purchase link:
www.smarturl.it/bookHaveBags

D.G. Kaye is back, and as she reflects on some of her more memorable vacations and travel snags, she finds herself constantly struggling to keep one step ahead of the ever-changing guidelines of the airlines—with her overweight luggage in tow. Her stories alert us to some of the pitfalls of being an obsessive shopper, especially when it comes time for D.G. to bring her treasures home, and remind us of the simpler days when traveling was a breeze.

In her quest to keep from tipping the scales, D.G. strives to devise new tricks to fit everything in her suitcases on each trip. Why is she consistently a target for Canada customs on her return journeys?

D.G.'s witty tales take us from airports, to travel escapades with best friends, to reflections on how time can change the places we hold dear in our hearts. Her memories will entertain and have you reminiscing about some of your own most treasured journeys—and perhaps make you contemplate revamping your packing strategies.